ONE – MADGE, IVAN & VERA

For much of my life I've worked in theatre, television or radio in one way or another. Often this has been alongside a 'day' job - the one that actually paid the bills.

I was born in Bristol to a distinctly non-theatrical family. My paternal family tended to live cheek by jowl in the terraces of Bristol's Barton Hill district gathering together for high days and holy days and no doubt doing their various party pieces by way of entertainment. I certainly recall my grandfather singing a music hall ditty entitled *I Can't Do My Bally Bottom Button Up* whilst puffing Woodbines and blowing the smoke out through his earholes. He didn't live to a great age, so I don't recommend it. They tended to work in the chocolate, tobacco and beer trades one way and another – so we certainly contributed to the crisis in the NHS. Sorry.

My maternal family are West Country and Welsh. My grandmother worked on Cardiff Market and my grandfather worked at Howell's, the city's leading department store, in the wireless and television department. He later taught at Brunel Technical College (where the exteriors for BBC's *Casualty* were filmed when it first aired). In 1958 the Empire Games (now the Commonwealth Games) were held in Cardiff with over 1,130 athletes competing from 36 countries and dependencies. My understanding is that my grandfather was responsible for playing the national anthems using a stack of LPs. He told me that the anthems were often terribly short, so each one was very hard to pin point accurately on the revolving vinyl record. This led to more than one occasion when the needle was dropped onto the neighbouring groove and the wrong anthem was broadcast to slightly puzzled athletes.

Each year my paternal grandparents took my sister, Anna, and I to the Bristol Hippodrome to see the pantomime. It's a fabulous theatre, opened in 1912 and designed by our foremost Edwardian theatre architect Frank Matcham. It's glorious inside – all red velvet and gold woodwork with a stunning central dome and almost two thousand seats. I well remember our visits to see John Inman, Danny La Rue, Cannon and Ball, The Krankies, Patrick Cargill, Victor Spinetti, Jeffrey Holland, Barry Howard, Ruth Madoc, Terry Scott and many more - little knowing that one day I'd get to cross paths with several of them. One year there was no pantomime. Instead, it was the touring production of *Annie* with Ursula Smith and Charles West. We were very disappointed - we wanted slosh scenes and a dame but actually, we loved it and for months afterwards we were still listening to the cassette tape of the score on a loop. Our poor mother. My love of theatre – and stage musicals - was born.

When I went to secondary school, I struck lucky. I had a fabulous drama teacher – Vera Connor. We did some interesting school plays – *She Stoops to Conquer, The Crucible, The Tinder Box* and several more – and I was in all of them, often alongside Adjoa Andoh, the deputy head's daughter and now, associate artist at the RSC. Vera pushed me to audition for drama school and she even stayed on a year after she should have retired to help me through my last twelve months.

We lived in a town at the southern end of the Cotswolds. One peopled with some colourful characters – Amy the singing road sweeper, Mr and Mrs Morley who ran a hardware shop stuffed with everything anyone could possibly want. One day. Wool shops with yellow film blinds on their windows which were lowered on sunny days to prevent the merchandise from fading. The Off License run by elderly Mrs Evans and her assistant, Rosemary, where I'd spend many an evening chatting away across a high glass counter decorated with bowls of dusty plastic grape bunches and delicately stacked Babycham bottles. The Georgian Boutique owned by Miss Vivian Partridge-New who was rather grand and took us under her wing determined to teach Anna and I elocution. Each week she took us through classics such as *The Lady of Shalott* or *Sir Galahad*. Happy days.

It was there that I joined the amateur dramatics society and took part on stage and off it. We were led by Marjorie Organ, known as Madge, who directed us, often drove us about, and who dedicated her life to theatre. Someone who also acknowledged Madge's help was actor Leslie Grantham. He was serving a term in prison at Leyhill, not that far from where we lived. Madge took Leslie under her wing and assisted him with preparing for auditions for drama school. Of course, he would later land the part of Dirty Den in *EastEnders*.

My dad started taking me into Bristol to see shows at the Colston Hall (now renamed Bristol Beacon) which contained several theatres. He also pulled strings to get me into the Bath Theatre Royal for a day of work experience. He managed the pub next to the theatre, the historic Garrick, and got chatting to actor Bill Owen (Compo in *Last of the Summer Wine*), who was appearing in panto, and who promised to have a word. So a few weeks later I spent the day with the company manager, and his dog, during a performance of *Hobson's Choice* starring Peter Vaughan, Stephanie Turner, Trevor Bannister and Ivan Beavis.

Ivan had played Harry Hewitt in *Coronation Street* and he took the time to chat to me about theatre and how important it was to get as much amateur experience as possible – and to have a second string to your bow. He also encouraged me to apply for drama school.

Eventually I did go off to study 'performing arts' in Yorkshire for two years. During this time, I decided that I didn't have what it took to become a professional actor but I did toy with the idea of becoming a newsreader. I had been asked to record some voice-overs for commercials shown on local cinema screens and the sound recordist remarked that he thought I had good diction and he was impressed by a couple of accents that I managed to do so, encouraged by him, I wrote to the BBC telling them what I thought I could do. They wrote back and told me what *they* thought I could do. So that was that. For a few years anyway.

Once graduated, I went to work in London. Firstly, for the drama school Mountview and then for British Telecom as an operator on the 999 service and finally for London Transport within the travel information department based opposite New Scotland Yard. I was basically a voice-over artiste recording travel information reports and updates that the public could telephone in and listen to. Long before the internet replaced us.

It was whilst doing this that I made the acquaintance of a chap who owned a small (very small actually) recording studio in central London. He asked me to record a voice-over for a theatre company who were touring schools with a play about road safety. I became the voice of the Belisha Beacon – Barney. Then I was asked to do some announcements for a circus and then a lift ... I know! Things were looking up – and down! Now the big one - I auditioned unsuccessfully to be the speaking clock – it wasn't my time. Over the years I've done everything from bumbling country yokels to RP cinema announcements about not rustling sweet wrappers.

I wanted to get back into theatre, so I moved to Manchester and eventually became Marketing Director of the famous Oldham Coliseum Theatre. That's when I got to work with many famous names – and I wrote my first book on the theatre's illustrious history. That led to getting involved in all kinds of extra-curricular activities – talking to groups, writing magazine articles, running events, looking after overseas *Coronation Street* fans, appearing on TV and radio ... and, well I'll fill you in a bit more as we go through this book.

Along the way I've met some wonderful characters. Many famous. Some infamous. Mostly, they're no longer with us. And some you won't have heard of at all – but all left a mark and, most importantly, a story to tell.

This book, this memoir, is not about me – but about the people I've met along the way and after all, it's the people we know that make us who we are. I hope that you will enjoy meeting them.

TWO – KENNY, ROY, JIMMIE & DORA

I was playing Dame Trot in an amateur pantomime at London's Bloomsbury Theatre. A friend of mine came back after a matinee performance to say that a famous actor was in the bar and wanted to meet me. When you play dame, you wear a lot of make-up, which I still had on, and I was somewhat exhausted with my feet up, so I wasn't keen to go out front -and I declined the invite. The name of the actor didn't mean anything to me to be honest – Ken Parry. However, I sent my best wishes and in due course I received a signed photo of said actor along with a scribbled note on the reverse giving his contact details and his unsolicited review of the show: 'The script was crap, but you were very good!' I'd written the script too.

I noted that this 'impertinent' thespian lived just a few streets away from me. At the time I was flat sharing in Clerkenwell, London and Ken lived in Myddleton Square, behind the Sadler's Wells Theatre. It was ten minutes away. I decided, a few weeks later, to pay him a visit. If only to defend my script!

Myddleton Square is a beautiful Georgian square with a church at its centre. Ken, or Kenny, or Mother Parry, or 'Camp-Parri', lived in the basement flat of one of these large houses. He was loud, large, northern, and a little intimidating in fact, especially when he adopted his trademark stance – hands on hips and flaring nostrils supporting heavy round glasses behind which beady eyes darted. He looked as if he'd stepped straight from the pages of a Dickens novel. A real-life Mr Bumble. With attitude. I climbed down the narrow stairs after being buzzed in. He was almost too large for the modest flat which had once been the servant's quarters of the impressive house. When he turned around in the kitchen it wasn't uncommon for crockery and cook books to cascade to the floor amid a tirade of salty curses.

Ken was a definite one-off. Born in Wigan in 1930 he'd started out working in a coal yard but, enchanted by a visit to the circus and in particular by a lady in a sparkling tutu atop a white pony by the name of Tishi, and haunted by the homophobic abuse from his fellow workers, he left home for the bright lights of London. When I first met him, he was playing the recurring role of 'Trolley Jack' in the Granada TV series *Children's Ward* hence his giving autographs to the children in my pantomime audience – they all knew him. His career had encompassed many highs – and quite a few lows. Amongst the highs were appearances with the RSC, at the National Theatre and the films *Spring and Port Wine* with James Mason, *Start the Revolution Without Me* with Gene Wilder, and *The Taming of the Shrew* with Richard Burton and Elizabeth Taylor. Ken insisted he'd had Miss Taylor round to the flat to teach her how to make gravy for Burton's Sunday lunches. It was probably true. He'd had that sort of life. He was full of tales and anecdotes.

On TV he'd appeared in *The Army Game, The Avengers, The Sweeney, The Young Ones, Dixon of Dock Green* and *Coronation Street* twice – as Rita's one-time agent Benny Stone and as the owner of the famed Orinoco Club, Sam Johnson. The flat was decorated with copious framed pictures of these productions, and he loved to talk about them and his career.

Ken had also been a 'mother' to a number of actors. Notably John Thaw, Mark Eden and Tom Courtney. That is to say that he'd given them lodgings and he'd nurtured their lives and careers. There was no doubt that Ken could be caring (he always used to boast 'I keep my friends in good order!') but he could also be hugely, and often hilariously, crass. Opposite the door to the lounge, for example, was the door to the loo and if he went in there for a call of nature, he would invariably leave the door open and stand there, trousers and pants round his rotund ankles, and continue the conversation with his guests as if it was quite normal.

Kenny had some wonderful stories. There's one that I always think of when I visit Blackpool. He was on tour with a theatre company by the glorious name of The Frank H Fortescue Famous Players and they were visiting the seaside resort. He and his fellow cast members weren't earning very much, and Ken was put in charge of booking some lodgings (or 'digs' as actors call them) at low cost. He found a suitable place and he and three of his cast mates checked in. They were immediately worried because the guest house was posher than they had expected – and in the front room, over the mantelpiece, was a big, framed portrait of the toothy film star George Formby. Agreeing that the high-earning performer must have lodged there Ken was urged by his mates to double-check the price of their stay. 'Mrs,' said a worried Ken to the landlady. 'How much is the board, only if Formby stays here ...' he said pointing to the portrait. 'Oh no,' she replied. 'He's never been here. I have that hanging there because my lad's a bit mucky, you know, and I've told him if he doesn't stop it, he'll end up looking like that ugly sod!'

He had appeared in an episode of *Nearest and Dearest*, the Granada TV comedy starring Hylda Baker and Jimmy Jewel, who hated each other. The two stars would check that they had the same number of lines and laughs in each script and there was a constant too-ing and fro-ing to the producer's office to report the other one. That producer was Bill Podmore, more of whom later, who enjoyed a drink, or three, and a laugh. One morning Hylda arrived in an unusually cheerful frame of mind. When she went to the toilet someone asked Bill if he knew what had perked her up. 'Oh,' he joked. 'I went round to her hotel last night and gave her one.' Parry's camp voice could be heard above the laughter: 'I can be difficult too you know.'

He was larger than life – perfect, one would have thought, for panto. But he didn't do many pantomimes. He once told me that he couldn't dance so playing the dame in one production, *Red Riding Hood* at Stratford East I think, he just couldn't get the hang of the comic striptease routine and the boys of the chorus had to whirl around him ripping his/her clothes off to the music. One review described it as watching Dame Dolly getting sexually assaulted by a group of gay rights campaigners. On the only other occasion, as far as I know, that he gave his dame he was delighted that his friend Welsh singing icon Dorothy Squires came to watch a matinee. Now, for younger readers, let me briefly explain that Dot, at one time married to Roger Moore, and one-time girlfriend of Mark Eden, was a brilliant Welsh singing star but she did like a drink, and she also had a very fiery temperament. She would threaten to sue anyone who said anything against her – so much so that she was banned from taking legal action eventually and branded a serial litigant. At this time, she was living in a huge mansion at Bexley in Kent

13

which would later burn to the ground. Her life was highly theatrical.

Anyhow, Dorothy and an entourage, turned up to watch Ken as Mother Goose at Palmer's Green, having had a few 'sherberts' en route. There came a scene in which Mother Goose was sitting on a milking stool shelling peas in a bucket. She did a 'woe is me' speech about how nobody loved her – and then Ken threw in an extra line about hoping to find a magical mansion in Bexley where someone still loved him. From the audience came a booming Welsh voice: 'You'll not be coming to my f***ing house – not after this performance!' Ken stomped to the front of the stage hands on hips: 'Oh yes I will Squires and what's more you'll damn well sing for me!' The row continued and the language got filthier and filthier. What the children in the audience thought we'll never know - but Ken never did a pantomime again.

Each year, on his birthday in June, he'd hold a lavish celebratory lunch, often as not at Rules in Covent Garden, known for its theatrical clientele. There would always be some sort of falling out between him and a guest or two. I attended on several occasions, and something always happened. Towards the end of his life, he became more infirm and he needed a mobility scooter (he ran over a man in a queue in Marks and Spencer's and then, when the man had been helped to his feet, did it again – only backwards!) and he became a frequent user of the Islington Council mobility bus scheme. This particular birthday, the guests were required to meet at the flat – they included myself, Dame Sian Phillips, Dame Eileen Atkins, Angus Lennie (who was abused for his present of wine: 'Don't go putting that cheap wine alongside my good stuff – it'll contaminate it'), Mark Eden,

Fenella Fielding, Michael Cashman, June Wyndham-Davies, and others. At the appointed hour, Ken mounted the new stair lift, and then made his way to the front door leading us all like a very loud pied piper.

Sian and I followed on arm in arm. The front door swung open and instead of seeing a fleet of waiting London cabs as we had expected, there was the council mobility bus. 'Oh,' someone said, 'They'll see us arriving!' Rules is frequented by actors, casting agents and producers and has a long frontage of glass windows. What everyone feared, of course, was that all these theatrical luminaries would see us arriving by council bus and wonder if we were all past it or fallen on hard times. 'It's alright, I'll get the driver to stop a little before the restaurant,' I promised.

To add insult to injury Ken boarded flourishing his free bus pass leaving the rest of us to pay a pound each. Sure enough the driver stopped short of the restaurant and we all climbed out, trooped past the Rules windows and entered without any embarrassment. That is until Parry, at the top of his voice, declared to Terry, who usually looked after us, 'Now then Dolly, let's get on with it - the mobility bus is booked to collect us at three!'

He would embarrass you at the drop of a hat – he announced loudly at an awards event that the only thing Judi Dench hadn't won was Crufts. I have no idea if she heard him, but she was just a few feet away from us at the time. At the opening of a West End show he dropped all his tablets on the floor of the Circle and abused the *EastEnders* cast for walking on them. 'Cough up me chuff and bark up me fringe!' was one of his favourite haranguing lines. I have no idea what it means but I still use it now and then.

Amongst Ken's career recollections were tales of his time in the ITV soap *Crossroads*: 'That was dreadful – I played Miss Diane's landlord, Leo Dolman, and I had to throw her out of her flat and of course, the programme was huge, and she was a very popular character. People were stopping me in the street and telling me off and this big thug even threatened to put my windows in.' Of *Start the Revolution Without Me*: 'Arthur Lowe and I were terrible laughers. For the close-ups the director had to put a board between us. The indignity!' Of his first agent: 'Oh yes, Joan Reddin. She promised me nothing – and kept her word!' Of the film *Burke and Hare*: 'Oh it was dreadful; I was the customer in a brothel and I had a nightshirt on and two poodles in my arms and all they wanted to do was get up me nightshirt the dirty buggers. Horrendous – never work with dogs love, never!' Of TV series *Thriller*: 'I was playing a taxi driver, but I couldn't drive, I couldn't do the pedals so I had this stunt man at my feet doing all that. Robert Lindsay was playing a policeman, and God love him, I almost knocked him down.' Of Alan Bennett: 'I bumped into him the other week and told him I'd pay for him to get over to Amsterdam, get high and sleep his way around the city. Perhaps that'll get this obsession with old ladies out of his system. He politely declined.'

We went out to dinner with actress Fenella Fielding one evening and she arrived late saying that she had been doing her hair. Fenella was a well-known wearer of wigs, so Kenny wasn't accepting the excuse. 'Why didn't you do what you normally do? Leave it in a bucket to soak overnight?' Fenella bridled, twinkled, and then burst out laughing. She'd been caught out and there was no arguing with Mother Parry.

He was also known for his psychic abilities. Sometimes these were sought out – Hollywood star Mae West called on him during a visit to London. As he once told me: 'This friend asked if I'd give her a reading – do you know, she came to the flat and ate all my Battenberg cake and ended up giving me a better reading than I'd given her. That's what you call a star!' Sometimes however he would have unsolicited visions. Once, he suddenly went into a trance pointing above my head and screaming that a dead butcher was there: 'You're going to have a change of career dear, did you always want to be a butcher?' I replied that nothing could be further from my thoughts. 'Well, suit yourself but the other side don't lie!' he rebuked me. I'm still waiting for the call of the cold meats counter.

Ken's proud boast was always that whoever came to visit his little basement flat invariably felt at home. 'Barely anyone sits in that chair without feeling so relaxed they doze off,' he used to say. They later discovered that he'd had a long-running minor gas leak.

I remember Christopher Biggins telling me a lovely tale of Parry. Ken was working on *The Taming of the Shrew* with Elizabeth Taylor in Italy when it was announced that Montgomery Clift had died. Taylor halted filming and took to her dressing room in grief. After an hour or so she returned to the set and apologised to everyone but explained that they were great friends and that they had been due to make a film together after this one. Parry piped up: 'Ah, have you thought of my friend Tom Courtney for the part?' Now, crass maybe – but he <u>was</u> also thinking of his friends.

Anyway, that's Ken. We became good friends, and I would call round and see how he was every few days. One evening he sat me down: 'Now love, I have a problem. I've got a friend staying here for a few weeks and I'm supposed to be cooking his tea and looking after him, but I've landed a film role and I'm going to have to go away for a few days.'

The film was a version of Chaucer's *The Miller's Tale* and there was one particular scene Ken was fretting over. 'You see, I die, and I fall to the floor and this lad then has it away with my daughter next to my dead body. I'm worried about doing it.' I offered consolation. 'Well, perhaps they won't actually need you to lie on the floor while they film that bit.' 'It's not that love, this boy is very good-looking and if I'm lying there when he gets his kit off, I shall want to get a good look. It's ... how do I die ... and keep one eye open?' That boy was/is Vincent Regan.

Roy Barraclough was the actor who was staying with Ken. He had left *Coronation Street* after playing Alec Gilroy, the miserly landlord of the Rovers Return, for a few years and now, having finished starring as Mother Goose at Wolverhampton, was rehearsing for the Leslie Bricusse musical *Sherlock Holmes* playing Dr Watson opposite Robert Powell as Sherlock. With Parry disappearing for a few days I, and my flat mate Paul, were drafted in to make sure Roy was fed.

Roy was very funny, very mischievous – and so, so down to earth. In fact, fame didn't rest easy with him. He used to say that an actor's job was to observe people and if the people were all looking at the actor, then you couldn't do it. He liked to blend into the background, liked to listen and liked the minimum of fuss. He also viewed acting as a job just like any other. He always referred to TV studios as 'sausage factories'

18

and he slightly resented working on TV because you are never in charge – there's always someone to add music, to alter the order, to cut a line, to leak the end of the story to the press. On stage it is you, the other actors and the audience. No one interferes.

Sherlock Holmes opened at the beautiful, and historic, Bristol Old Vic. In fact, it's the oldest continually working theatre in the country. Then it embarked on a national tour. I was able to meet up with Roy now and again and enjoyed watching the show several times. There was one song in it called *I Shall Find Her*. Sherlock's love interest has been kidnapped and the cast criss-cross the stage supposedly looking for her with lyrics like 'I shall find her – in a courtyard, in a house, in a hallway, in ...' whatever. Roy would change the lyrics if he knew I was listening to absurd ones like 'I shall find her in a toilet, up a chuff, in a dunny, feeling rough!' That's when Roy and I began our relationship which would last over a quarter of a century - until his death in 2017.

The tour of *Sherlock Holmes* actually finished early as the producers were having financial difficulties. The last date was the stunning Blackpool Grand, one of Roy's favourite theatres and where he and Les Dawson had enjoyed a long and successful summer season – and where Roy had appeared in pantomime more than once. And where today there is a seat bearing his name. Les and his wife Tracy attended the opening night with Les declaring in the bar afterwards: 'The only thing that will kill this show is word of mouth!' Les confided in Roy that they'd been asked to reprise their Cissie and Ada act as a sitcom and the pair agreed to meet for lunch later in the week to discuss the details.

The next day Les was having routine medical tests and he died in the hospital room. As Roy was driving to the Grand Theatre that night he heard the news on the radio, the press were waiting at the stage door to get his reaction. He collapsed in his dressing room, but he couldn't disappoint a sell-out audience, so he battled the tears and delivered another stellar performance as Dr Watson.

As Les left us so Jimmie Chinn arrived. When *Sherlock Holmes* was playing Wimbledon Jimmie turned up at the stage door asking to speak with Roy. He explained that when Roy had been a member of the theatrical company at Oldham in the 1960s Jimmie had been to every play and had come to admire Roy's work. Jimmie had written for *Emmerdale Farm* (as it was then called) for a time and had written copious radio plays and even had a West End hit with his play *Straight and Narrow*. He told Roy that he was sorry he hadn't wanted to do a play he'd written for him some years earlier entitled *A Different Way Home*. Roy had no recollection of seeing such a script but he offered to read it. Jimmie had brought along a copy just in case and Roy promised to let him know what he thought.

A few weeks later, one evening, after a performance, we were eating fish and chips when Roy remembered the play. It was a one-hander, just one character called Leslie who still lived with his mother in Oldham. The play, which ran to about half an hour or so, saw Leslie tell the story of his life and ended with the death of his mother. It was beautiful – funny, warm – and painfully sad. We both knew that the script was something special but at only half an hour it wasn't long enough to make it onto the stage. But Roy knew he had to perform it.

At the time Granada were in negotiations for him to star in a new sit-com by the wonderful writer John Stevenson. Called *Mother's Ruin* it centred on a health food shop run by an over-bearing mother and her son (Roy). Dora Bryan would end up playing the mother. Anyway, he used the discussions to insist that Granada had to let him record *A Different Way Home*.

He filmed it in front of a studio audience – not using autocue but having learnt the whole thing. He did two takes and I sat with Jimmie to watch it. It was broadcast in the Granada region only late on Christmas Eve, stuck in a slot where very few would have watched but something extraordinary happened – literally hundreds of letters flooded in. Those who watched it loved it; it mirrored something which had happened in their family, to them, to a neighbour. At the heart of the story was the fact that Leslie had stayed at home to look after his mother whilst his sister Maureen had married and moved away. The night mum had gone into hospital to die, Leslie had sat by her side hour after hour until a kindly nurse suggested he go home for a couple of hours' rest. He'd just got home when the telephone rang – mum had died. She had looked at the nurse and, in her last words, called her Maureen. So many viewers wrote to say that they too had left a loved one's bedside for a short time only to miss the last few minutes. Roy also had letters from medical professionals attesting to the fact that this often happened – almost as if the dying often needed to be alone for the final farewell. The reaction was such that we knew something more had to happen with *A Different Way Home.*

And it did. Roy suggested to Jimmie that he write some more material for Leslie. That would form the first half of the play. They then decided that Maureen, the sister, should speak. She should tell the same story but from her point of view. So, at the end of Act One your heart breaks for this poor man. Then in Act Two Maureen arrives and she has the whole of the second act to tell her side – and then we realise why she's there, in the family home. Leslie has died and she's waiting alone for the hearse. Roy suggested they ask Lynda Barron to play Maureen but someone, I can't remember who, said 'No,' and the crazy idea was that Roy should play her as well. And that's what was decided upon.

It was premiered at the Oldham Coliseum Theatre, and it sold out, had rave reviews, and won a number of awards including best production and best actor. Some London producers came to see it and there was talk of it going into the West End however Roy was under contract to *Coronation Street* and in the storyline, Alec had gone off for a few weeks on a cruise ship and was due back behind the bar so taking the play to London was out of the question and thus back to Granada TV he went. A lot of his friends and fellow Corrie cast had come to see the show. I remember Liz Dawn (Vera Duckworth in Corrie) asking me where the tele-prompter was. She couldn't comprehend that Roy had managed to learn two hours' worth of script. Julie Hesmondhalgh, who had not long joined the cast as Hayley, came – what a delight she was and she remains a good friend to this day.

A few years later, when Roy had left Corrie for good, he toured *A Different Way Home* around the country and again it was well received and garnered lots of fan letters telling their stories of bereavement and loss. It really is a special piece.

Jimmie Chinn was brought up in Middleton in the borough of Rochdale, an only child, raised by his single-parent mother Edie. Jimmie's writing invariably reflects that upbringing and many of their friends and neighbours are mentioned - often by name - in his works. After leaving school Jim worked at the local Co-op and got involved with several am-dram societies – most notably the Curtain Theatre in Rochdale. By then he was also making weekly visits to the Oldham Coliseum (known as the 'Rep' in those days) to see a play every week. He even got to appear there – as an extra in *The Scarlet Pimpernel*. At the age of 19 he left for London having gained a scholarship for RADA and studied alongside John Alderton, Tom Courtenay, John Thaw and Sarah Miles. As he would put it – he had a short-lived career as an actor – becoming a teacher and then a writer. His mother came to see him act just once. He was in a play called *The Paragon*. Jimmie told me: 'I have to admit that it was dreadful, but I remember asking my mother afterwards if she'd enjoyed it and all she said was that she was horrified at how much whiskey I was drinking. She was embarrassed to see me drunk in public. I couldn't persuade her that it was just cold tea, and I was acting.'

One of the delights of knowing Jimmie was going to a café or restaurant with him. He would take everything in – all the people, all their characteristics – and he'd invent lots of little plays there and then. 'Look at that old lady there with her son. He's left his wife Shirley back home in Leamington Spa and he's come up here to take his old mum out to lunch. He's tried to talk her into selling the house and moving into a care home but she's not for it. Ah, isn't that lovely. Mind you, when he drops her home, he's planning to do her in. Shirley's already sold the house from under her you see and the new people are moving in next month so needs must. And over there – Bob and Glenda out for Sunday lunch. Mind you, she's been stealing from the church for years and he's not noticed because he's having an affair with the verger. They're all as bad as each other.'

Jimmie had a lot of stories – here's a favourite. He was working as an usher in the Empire in Leicester Square and *Dr Zhivago* was showing. An elderly, rather grand, lady would buy a ticket for almost every showing but when the big snow scene began she'd put an umbrella up and sit there. People behind her, obviously, took umbrage and one day Jimmie had to go and speak with her. He asked her, very politely, to take the umbrella down. 'Are you mad? In this weather?' She replied.

The first of Jimmie's plays I ever saw produced was *Straight and Narrow* in the West End, long before I actually knew him, starring Nicholas Lyndhurst, Carmel McSharry, Anna Keaveney and Melanie Kilburn. The next was the premiere of *Sylvia's Wedding* starring Lynette McMorrough, Sally-Anne Matthews, Norman Rossington and Freddie Pyne. *Straight and Narrow* was his big hit but there are many, many more. Roy appeared in several of his radio plays including a trio with Bernard Cribbins and Dora Bryan. Jimmie also wrote 37 episodes of *Emmerdale*. There was also a film script – *Farewell Performance* – which was to have starred Elizabeth Taylor and Sir John Gielgud, but Taylor was taken ill, and it fell through sadly. Have you noticed how the same people keep cropping up? Small world, isn't it?

Many of the characters in Jimmie's plays are held within their own worlds, frightened of other people, what people might think of them, worried that they might step out of line or out of their class. Scared of the outside world, scared that they might show themselves up. Maybe Jimmie had a little bit of that in him too – I remember him staying with us, which he did quite a lot, for the first time. For some reason we had to go out and leave him in the house for an afternoon on his own. When we came home, he asked why we'd left all the surveillance cameras on. He had been upset that we were filming him, perhaps not trusting him in our home, and he had sat in one room and hadn't dared move. We explained that they were the motion-detector alarm sensors which flashed a red light– but they weren't recording him. That was Jimmie. Sadly, he died in 2011 and I think of him every day.

I'm going to go back to *Mother's Ruin* now – the Sunday teatime series which Roy did with Dora, Jason Done, Kay Adshead and Julia Deakin. It's fair to say that it wasn't a huge success. John Stevenson's idea was that it should be a throwback to the old sitcoms – *Nearest and Dearest, In Loving Memory* and so on - but the critics weren't up for it. The cast rehearsed in London and I often went along to the rehearsal room to watch as I was still living in the capital at the time and working for London Transport. There was one episode which featured a funeral and a gathering of the clans – amongst the guest actors were Alan Rothwell (one of the original cast of *Coronation Street* playing Ken's brother David Barlow) and Kenneth Alan Taylor (Ken would later direct the Oldham production of *A Different Way Home*) who played Cecil Newton, owner of Newton and Ridley on TV.

Kenneth introduced me to his real-life actress wife Judith Barker who had played Ken Barlow's second wife, Janet. A small soap world, isn't it? Both Kenneth (known as KAT) and Judith would play big parts in my life in the near future. But, for now, let's linger on Dora Bryan.

If you're too young to remember Dora please look her up - what a character and what a legend! I loved to sit and chat with her in her dressing room and we, and her ex-cricketer husband Bill, quickly became friends. Dora was born in Parbold, Lancashire but raised in Oldham under her real name Dora Broadbent. It was Noel Coward who encouraged her to change her name when she was cast in the West End premiere of his play *Private Lives*. She told me that she was inspired by a box of Bryant and May matches – and became Dora Bryant but an error was made in the printing of some posters and the name was inadvertently shortened from Bryant to Bryan. In reality her married name was Dora Lawton.

Dora's film, TV and stage credits is a stunning list – *A Taste of Honey, The Blue Lamp, The Sandwich Man, Carry On Sergeant, Dinnerladies, Last of the Summer Wine*, and on stage, *Hello, Dolly!, 70 Girls 70, Charley Girl, Pygmalion* …. the list goes on. She was also known as 'Dizzy Dora' and was always involved in some kind of mishap and confusion. There's the story of her starring in *Hello, Dolly!* in Manchester. Taking a walk around the city one day she decided to see a show, so she called in at the theatre box office and asked what was on. 'You!' they replied. She had forgotten that she had a matinee. Maybe apocryphal. Maybe true, knowing Dora.

She and Bill lived in Brighton, in the basement flat of a lovely seafront property that they had once owned and run as a hotel. They had got into financial trouble and had to sell the place just keeping the basement for themselves. They would arrive at the Coliseum Theatre, where I was now working, without any warning. One day I got a call from the box office to inform me that Miss Bryan was in the foyer looking for me. She explained that she and Bill had decided to drive up north on a whim, had checked into a hotel somewhere and had come to visit me. In her hand was a large glass of red wine. Now, Dora struggled with drink, so I asked her where she'd got it from. 'Well, I don't know – this man just came up to me in the street and said I should have it!'

Things got worse when neither she nor Bill could recall the name of the hotel they'd supposedly checked into or indeed, where it was. The room key had an anonymous fob on it and numerous calls to local hotels drew a blank, so they came to stay with us minus their luggage. We never did find out where they'd been. Or whether it was true. Or whether they got their luggage back.

She used to tell stories, against herself, of some of the crazy things that had happened. She was cast in the West End production of *The Full Monty* – as a musical with the action relocated from Sheffield to Buffalo, USA. I know! Dora played the elderly pianist (which she did with a Lancastrian accent a lot of the time). All didn't go well in rehearsals. One day her mobile telephone started ringing and the director was furious and threatened to fine her. She handed the thing over explaining that she didn't know how to silence it. The next day she produced the 'phone from her handbag and plonked it on the director's table. He informed her that this was a TV remote control. 'Oh heck,' she said. 'Bill will be trying to watch the cricket with my mobile!'

When the show opened, things stayed the same. During one performance, on a whim and mid-scene, she addressed the audience to let them know that she and Thora Hird had been to the Chelsea Flower Show! Eventually she left the show and Lynda Barron stepped in. She told me that she hadn't liked it anyway: 'They keep singing and then getting their willies out darling.'

One of my favourite stories, which she used to tell, was of her being a guest speaker on a cruise ship. They docked for the day in Malaga, Spain and she went off to buy a travel kettle for her cabin so that she could make her own tea. She ended up in the department store *El Corte Ingles* which had ferocious air-conditioning, so she took a cardigan off a hanger and put it over her shoulders. She got her kettle and a few other bits and went to the tills. She paid for her purchases but of course, forgot about the cardigan so as she tried to leave the alarms went off. There was a kerfuffle – not helped by 'Dizzy Dora' I shouldn't think! Anyway, as Dora used to tell it she ended up in the security office and then the police were called, and she was taken to the police station. 'I kept telling them who I was but not a flicker,' she explained. 'I told them I was a national treasure and I ended up doing the splits and singing three choruses of *Hello, Dolly* but they'd never heard of me!' Eventually she was taken to the ship in a police car where the captain had to sign for her on the quayside. She was escorted back to her cabin where she plugged the kettle in to make a restorative cuppa – fusing the cabin.

When she was starring in *The Birthday Party* at the National Theatre I went to watch the show. She knew that I was in the audience, and she'd promised to make a sign to let me know that she knew - if you see what I mean. *The Birthday Party* is a very serious piece and she was acting opposite Trevor Peacock. Every time there was a pause (which there's a lot of in Harold Pinter's works) I saw her look out into the vast auditorium trying to locate me and my heart went into my mouth imagining her about to wave. Lucky, she didn't. After the performance we went to the bar and she told me that the last time she'd appeared at the National, which has several performance spaces within it, she was playing in a restoration comedy with a big wig featuring a galleon. She'd got confused backstage and had made an entrance into the wrong theatre startling the cast of the modern comedy which was in full flow at the time.

She sort of did the same thing at West Yorkshire Playhouse when she was appearing in the lovely Alan Bennett *Talking Heads* plays in one of their theatres. In the other Edward Fox was doing a Terence Rattigan set in a headmaster's study. The plays started at different times and when the Rattigan stage management team checked their set prior to curtain up they found Dora sat on stage, in the panelled room set, eating her sandwiches. She thought it was the Green Room bless her.

I loved the story her son Daniel told at her funeral – his mother rang to say that she'd crashed the car into the front of a charity shop. But all was not lost – she'd found a lovely blouse in there! Dora was just fabulous.

It was during the recording of *Mother's Ruin* that I also met legendary *Coronation Street* producer Bill Podmore for the first time along with writer John Stevenson, who remained a good friend until his death in 2023. Bill liked a drink, so it was appropriate that I met them in the Granada bar with Bill introducing John as 'the end of the pier Oscar Wilde!' John wrote for *Coronation Street* between 1976 and 2006 and he came up with some wonderful stories. I recall him telling me that his own mother, who lived in Saddleworth just outside Oldham, had taken up driving late in life. One day she was setting out in bad weather to visit friends and she had an accident skidding off the road and into a ditch. Unperturbed she abandoned the car unwilling to make a fuss or, more importantly, miss the lunch. This led to a storyline with Annie Walker taking up driving lessons and crashing into Stan Ogden's window cleaning cart – and of course, the famous scene with Fred, Bet and Betty taking Annie's Rover for a drive and ending up in a lake. Incidentally, Julie Goodyear told me that when they were filming that at a Cheshire stately home, they drove into the lake, the car started to fill with water and then the director announced it was lunch break. The crew went off to eat leaving the actors in the car in the lake (their bottom halves wrapped in bin bags) until they all came back to continue shooting. But more of Julie later.

John's credits include co-creation of, and co-writing, the fabulous *Brass* which starred Tim West, *The Brothers McGregor* which was inspired by two characters he created in Corrie (and which Ken Dodd told John one evening when we were all together was one of the funniest shows he'd seen – not a bad compliment missus) and *The Last of the Baskets* amongst other things.

John would often discuss potential *Coronation Street* story ideas when we went out to dinner. One evening we discussed the idea that Rita and Alec might grow closer. We chatted about how this would happen and why Rita would let down her defences. The result was the idea that Rita would suffer an illness which would cause her to need Alec's help. A

30

story which involved Rita suffering carbon monoxide poisoning from a faulty gas fire was the result. At first, she didn't know what was making her ill and Alec looked after her which eventually led to Alec and Rita becoming engaged. A Christmas wedding was mooted but Roy had already decided to leave the show, so Rita never became Rita Gilroy. That storyline, incidentally, also led to an increase in sales of carbon monoxide alarms across the UK.

John would often bemoan the lack of credit the writers enjoyed, and he would tell a lovely tale about Arthur Lowe, who was starring in John's series *The Last of the Baskets*. It co-starred Ken Jones as a factory worker who inherited the title Earl of Clogborough, a castle and a manservant, Bodkin, in the shape of Arthur. One day at rehearsals Arthur invented a little bit of comedy business to enhance a scene and wishing to show off a tad he proclaimed to producer Bill Podmore: 'We don't need a writer, do we Bill?' Bill looked at Arthur and replied: 'Of course we don't Arthur. Not once we've got the script!'

John died in September, 2023. Sarah Lancashire (John created the character of Raquel Wolstenholme), producer Mervyn Watson and John's often-time writing collaborator Julian Roach (who himself wrote for the show for 27 years) all delivered tributes at his funeral. John wrote 447 *Coronation Street* episodes and around 200 episodes of other shows. He was one of the nicest people I've ever known. Something funny happened as I left the crematorium – something I think John would have enjoyed. I'd been stood by Bill Roache in the line to leave and we were bemoaning the fact that we didn't go to many christenings and weddings any more – it was all-too often funerals. As we stepped outside an undertaker, who knew me, waved – I knew him as a local councillor. 'Oh,' said Bill. 'Yes, you must come to quite a few!'

Another little diversion. Ken Morley was appearing at the Alexandra Theatre in Birmingham and turned up on the first day to move into his dressing room. The stage door keeper, a doddery old chap, led him along the meandering backstage corridors and then down some narrow steps to this little, desolate dressing room. 'Oh, it's lovely!' said Ken sarcastically. 'I know,' replied the chap. 'We've had 'em all here – in fact one of your colleagues used this one. Arthur Lowe!' Ken explained that Arthur was in Corrie long before he was – but that he was a fan of Arthur's work. 'Good – you'll enjoy it in here then - he died in that chair!' came the dead-pan response as the chap closed the door behind him.

THREE – TONY, THE COBBLES & THE CAST

My paternal grandparents lived in a council tower block in Bristol. In one corner of the lounge sat their most prized possession – well, it wasn't theirs actually, it was rented from Rediffusion. But there sat the TV. If you wanted to change the channel you had to turn a dial mounted on the wall and every night they watched Michael St John, the HTV West continuity announcer who always sported a fresh carnation, give a cheeky wink and wish them goodnight before the national anthem was played. Then my grandfather would switch the thing off, wait for it to cool down and place a tablecloth over it for the night. It was the most valuable thing in the flat.

The first episode of *Coronation Street* that I can recall watching on that set went out on 7th March, 1979. We watched along with almost 17 million others, around a third of the UK population at the time. One of the plots that evening had Deirdre Langton taking two-year-old Tracy, who was in her pushchair, for a stroll. As they passed the Rovers Deirdre decided to pop in and see Annie Walker leaving Tracy outside for a few minutes. Bet was serving Len, Mike and Alf and directed Deirdre to the back room where Annie showed her some knitting. She was making Tracy a gift. As they exchanged a few words there was an almighty crash. A builder's lorry had turned over outside the pub and dozens of planks of wood had cascaded through the pub windows.

Inside, Alf and Mike were injured. But where was Tracy? Poor Anne Kirkbride, as Deirdre, had to film for two days shouting Tracy's name over and over amid the wreckage, smoke and dust. In those scenes she conveyed the trauma of a mother desperate to find her child. I always say that soap actors have to, largely, act from the shoulders up. It's very often all we see of them in major storylines. Annie Kirkbride could do it with less than that – her neck did the lot. Deirdre spent quite a while wandering desolately around the Castlefield area of Manchester contemplating her life but luckily, it being soap opera, Tracy turned out to have been kidnapped only moments before the crash. The pair were happily reunited on a canal bank. A lot of Corrie drama takes place on canal sides - had you noticed? You may also ruminate that had Tracy actually perished in 1979 it might have saved a lot of *Coronation Street* residents a fair bit of misery at her hands over the next few decades. And, as someone once said – Tracy Barlow – even her initials are a killer disease.

The next episode I vividly recall was shown on 28th July, 1980. It also featured an accident and a lorry. Alf Roberts had been teaching wife Renee to drive but he'd had enough and refused to give her another lesson. However, they headed into the country for a pub lunch. Alf had too much to drink and was forced to allow Renee to drive them home. Needs must and all that. On a remote country road, she stalled the engine in the middle of a contraflow and panicked. Alf climbed out to go round and take over the wheel. With him out of the vehicle, but Renee still in the driving seat, a lorry appeared from the opposite direction and smashed head on into the stationary car. The last shot of the episode was Renee, splattered in blood, eyes wide open.

Both of those episodes were written by HV Kershaw and both demonstrated great acting, superb stunt work and high drama set against comedy. That's what set *Coronation Street* apart. I've just re-watched both of those episodes and they still stand up today.

Coronation Street went on air for the first time in December, 1960 and quickly became the flagship show from the Granada Television stable. Of course, Granada built up an impressive roster of hits from *Brideshead Revisited* to *The Jewel in the Crown*, *Sherlock Holmes* to *The Royale Family, World in Action* to *The Krypton Factor*, which I actually made a brief non-speaking appearance on in one episode. Not doing the assault course I can assure you!

Granada was owned by brothers Sidney and Cecil Bernstein. It got its name from one of their favourite holiday destinations, the city of Granada in Spain, famous for the Moorish Alhambra Palace. In 1934 their business became Granada Limited and was listed on the stock market a year later. The business they were in was cinemas.

In 1953 the government announced the auction of franchises for a new network of commercial television stations. The Bernsteins decided to bid for the London region, where they were based, but that they were tipped off that so many companies were also doing so that they were unlikely to win. They then looked at rainfall maps and settled on the northern England region thanks to the amount of likely bad weather. Rain, they concluded, would likely keep people at home. Watching their channel. In 1954 they were awarded the Monday-Friday North of England franchise (ABC won the weekend equivalent) covering a whole swathe of the country from Merseyside to Yorkshire.

'The north and London were the two biggest regions. Granada preferred the north because of its tradition of home-grown culture, and because it offered a chance to start a new creative industry away from the metropolitan atmosphere of London ... the north is a closely knit, indigenous, industrial society; a homogeneous cultural group with a good record for music, theatre, literature, and newspapers, not found elsewhere in this island, except perhaps in Scotland. Compare this with London and its suburbs — full of displaced persons. And, of course, if you look at a map of the concentration of population in the north and a rainfall map, you will see that the north is an ideal place for television,' wrote Sidney Bernstein.

The Bernsteins toured the area looking for a suitable site on which to build their studios (the headquarters were always in London) focusing on Manchester and Leeds. Eventually land at Quay Street, right in the heart of Manchester, was purchased for £82,000 and architect Ralph Tubbs, whose best-known work at this period had been the Dome of Discovery for the Festival of Britain, was engaged to design studios and offices. The studios themselves were named 2, 4, 6 and 8 which was said to have been so that their rival broadcasters would assume they had more studios than they actually did. These were the first purpose-built TV studios in the UK pre-dating the BBC's Television Centre by five years.

Granada first went on air on 3rd May, 1956 but the cost of building the studios and the assembling of its workforce was already threatening to bring the company to the brink of insolvency. In 1968 there was a reorganisation of franchises and that's when Granada was given a seven-day license, but the price was that it give up the territory east of the Pennines and this led to the launch of Yorkshire Television.

It was of course Tony Warren who created *Coronation Street* for Granada. Not that that was his real name. Anthony McVeigh Simpson was born in Salford in 1936. The Simpsons lived at Wilton Avenue in Pendlebury and Tony would attend Eccles Grammar School. His father, who spoke several languages, was often away buying up fruit and vegetables for the Manchester markets. As such Tony was brought up in a matriarchal household and he once told me that he loved to sit under the tablecloth-draped table in the best room when his mum came back from church with her friends. Here he could listen to all the gossip, which would come in handy during his writing years.

Tony was a child actor using Warren as his stage name. He frequently worked for BBC Radio often alongside Violet Carson (later Ena Sharples), Doris Speed (Annie Walker) and Alan Rothwell (David Barlow). *Children's Hour* producer Trevor Hill recalled Tony as 'An excitable young teenager' and it has gone down in Corrie history that Violet Carson once threatened to smack his bottom if he didn't calm down. There's also the tale of Vi singing a song called *Bowton's Yard* to him. She told the story herself on his *This Is Your Life* in 1995 of how this song, she thought, might have inspired him to create *Coronation Street*. *Bowton's Yard* was a song Vi recorded and it takes the lyrics of a local dialect poem by Samuel Laycock about the neighbours living in a yard in Victorian Stalybridge. Tony himself recalled first hearing it: 'Violet slid off a few knuckles full of rings, sat down at the piano and played *Bowton's Yard*. I was transfixed.' The real, infamous, yard itself was demolished in 1937 and a petrol station now stands on the site.

His producer on *Children's Hour,* Olive Shapley also recalled sharing a train journey with him: 'At about Crewe, after a long period of silence, Tony suddenly woke me up saying, 'Olive, I've got this wonderful idea for a television series. I can see a little back street in Salford, with a pub at one end and a shop at the other, and all the lives of the people there, just ordinary things and ...' I looked at him blearily and said 'Oh. Tony, how boring! Go back to sleep' ... Tony has never let me forget my error of judgement.'

He later went to drama school in Liverpool but spent much of his time at Manchester's imposing and romantic Central Library, built to echo the design of the Parthenon in Rome, reading theatrical and film autobiographies. Eventually he ended up in London and unable to secure acting work returned home in 1959 at the age of 23. Incidentally, Ken Parry, who I recalled in the previous chapter claimed that he leant Tony the fare to get home – and that he never got it back. Tony went along to Granada looking for a suitable casting opportunity but was pointed instead in the direction of Harry Elton.

Harry was the Executive Producer for Dramas and Serials and had worked for Granada since 1957 having relocated from his native Canada. Harry took a chance and engaged Tony to write scripts for, amongst other things, *Biggles* and *Shadow Squad*. According to Tony his heart wasn't in it. He once told me that everything was too posh and he longed to write about Salford and Manchester people, the people and places he knew best. Eventually things came to a head and Harry told him to go home and write about the area he knew - but he only had 24 hours to come up with a script and he was warned that 'It had better take Britain by storm.'

On the wall of Tony's bedroom hung a print of an illustration from the story *Sleeping Beauty*. It was of Prince Florizel cutting his way through the undergrowth to reach Beauty in her castle. Tony took inspiration and named the street he was going to write about *Florizel Street*. 'Only a gay man could have written it,' he used to say. A pub at one end with a strong woman in charge, Annie Walker. A shop at the other again with a woman at the reigns in Florrie Lindley. Seven houses in between with Elsie Tanner right in the middle. And across the road, the Glad Tidings Mission, with Ena Sharples ruling the roost. The show was always about strong women for women viewers.

Tony delivered his script and Harry loved it. Eventually it went in front of the board for their approval. It wasn't forthcoming.

Victor Peers, Granada's General Manager, said of the initial script: 'There is not a single thing I like about this programme. I don't like the settings or the characters or the way they talk to each other.'

Denis Forman: 'Your show is neither funny enough on the one hand nor documentary enough on the other. People won't know what to make of it.'

Eddie Pola declared it to be 'Crap.'

Sidney Bernstein: 'Harry, when I get driven in from the airport, I see many houses that are much nicer than those on your street. Is this the image of Granadaland we want to project to the rest of the country?'

His bother Cecil: 'You've made a horrible mistake, and we can't blame you because you are a Canadian.'

Harry Elton himself recorded: 'With a rare show of unanimity the committee had decided this programme was not what it wanted to put on air.' However, they had airtime to fill and Harry informed his bosses that there was nothing else in the pipeline. Very reluctantly they gave the go-ahead for *Florizel Street* to have a run of 13 episodes and decreed that the street should be demolished in the last one.

A cast was assembled with a couple of late changes here and there. Such as Nita Valerie being replaced by Vi Carson as Ena, the addition of the character of Uncle Albert, the Barlow's having two sons instead of a son and a daughter ... and the addition of the famous hairnets for Ena (though Vi Carson would wear two or three in most episodes so that they showed up better on camera according to then Granada publicist Leita Donn). The other major change was the name of the street, and therefore the show. Harry recorded a pilot episode which he played on monitors around the studios asking staff to complete questionnaires rating casting, storylines and so on. The response was positive, but a tea lady asked why the show had the name of a disinfectant. A new name had to be found.

There's a fictional history of the street but at the beginning it was a slightly moveable feast and there was much debate as to when the street would have been built. Two possible years were considered – 1897, a Jubilee year, and 1902, a Coronation year. They were the choices for the show's name. At a boozy dinner the executives were asked to vote with the result taken back to Granada to be 'phoned through to London. It's said that the secretary carrying out this task saw what they'd settled on and decided that they'd made the wrong choice so she 'phoned through with her pick – *Coronation Street*. I hope it's true.

On Friday 9th December, 1960 the first episode was broadcast live. It was snowing so the viewing figures were good. It wasn't yet, however, a national transmission. That came in March, 1961. Lew Grade was the owner of ATV, one of the networks which declined to take Corrie from the beginning, but his wife, Kathleen, visited her parents that Christmas at their home in Hulme, Manchester. She saw the show and persuaded her husband to put it on his stations. He agreed but only if it moved from 7pm to 7.30pm. Instead of the bulldozers moving onto *Coronation Street* at the end of the 13 episodes Granada, slightly puzzled by its success, gave the green light to keep it on air.

The conveyor belt now had to be fed. Tony once told me that the success, though welcome, now led to him losing control of his baby. He wrote the first 12 episodes with HV Kershaw writing a new 13th one designed to keep the show going. A team of writers was assembled which included, in those early months, Alick Hayes, Wyn Davies, John Alldridge, Harry Driver, Vince Powell, Michael Dines, John Finch, Alan Prior and Jack Rosenthal. Tony wrote a further 69 episodes over a 16-year period but his baby now had foster parents and he found that transition difficult. He also slightly resented the attitude to the actors telling me that he regularly saw the public flocking to meet the cast while he stood aside unrecognised. 'I used to think, hang on – I created them! Don't you want to meet me?'

He did have another series made by Granada. It was called *The War of Darkie Pilbeam*, a three-part wartime drama centred on a black marketer played by Trevor Bannister, broadcast in 1968. Amongst the cast were some familiar Corrie names including Lynne Carol (Martha Longhurst), Roy Barraclough (Alec Gilroy), Julie Goodyear (Bet Gilroy), Christine Hargreaves (Christine Hardman), George Waring (Arnold Swain) and Alan Browning (Alan Howard). It was produced by Richard Everitt.

Everitt had joined Granada in 1960 initially as a floor manager for the series *Biggles*. He became the man who would cue the start of that very first episode of *Coronation Street* and although his career included working on dozens of shows and becoming a much-lauded director he also played a big part in Corrie's ongoing development. In 1965 he became producer and in 1967 took over as Executive Producer. It was Richard who urged the building of the show's first proper outdoor set. One of my prized possessions is his original dossier, from 1967, in which he developed his plans for the show (another is set of Hilda's flying ducks given to me by producer Bill Podmore as the paint was flaking off them). These included Emily getting married and moving away (not actually carried through), Ena becoming 'more bitchy', plans to bring back Elsie's toughness, and the introduction of a Marxist character.

The really big change in 1968 though was the creation of the show's first outdoor set, or 'the lot' as it became known. Until then the street set was inside with the house frontages made of wood and canvas and the cobbles painted on the floor. The writers tended to pen scenes for one end of the street or the other as it was difficult to fit the whole of the street set plus the interiors into the studio at any one time. In 1965 no.7 collapsed and until 1982, when Len Fairclough built a new house there, the plot remained empty apart from a bench. This was in fact partly written into the scripts so as to allow the set to be shunted together a little bit.

In 1967 a train crashed over the viaduct and a real fire engine had to be used in studio but due to the restrictions of the indoor set, the lack of space and the fact that the house frontages were each only about six feet wide, the crash episodes were highly complicated to film. This led to Richard Everitt being tasked with finding somewhere to film outside. The answer was right under their noses. Between the studio building and the Victorian Bonded Warehouse, which was used for rehearsals, sat a small railway sidings with cobbles and a viaduct. This was rented from British Railways and the indoor set simply moved outdoors and plonked on the siding's existing cobbles, which incidentally ran diagonally across the street – something which never happened in real streets.

The first episode to feature the new lot was broadcast on 24th January, 1968 – but we only saw the demolition of the Glad Tidings Mission. Viewers had to wait until April to see some of the terraced side of the street. The following year the houses were re-enforced and made more realistic by the addition of brick walls and partial slate roofs. Jean Alexander (Hilda Ogden) remembered it as 'the coldest place on earth.' It was still not full sized. In 1981 work began on a replacement just a short distance away, the other side of the Bonded Warehouse, still within the studio complex. This opened in 1982 and there were some additions – Len built that new house at no.7 and a gate was added between the Rovers and Uncle Albert's. Up until then customers using the toilet in the pub opened the door straight into Uncle Albert's front room. No wonder he was so grumpy! And the walls of the back yards were made of plastic brick so they could be removed allowing a crew to be in one yard filming the cast in another.

In 2013 the show moved to the current set at Media City. This became the first full-sized lot the show had ever had and now features buildings from the wider Weatherfield area – the precinct, police station and so on. The old Quay Street sets are long gone but many memories transferred to the Quays such as the old cobbles, actually setts, now on Victoria Street, and the door handles from the old Rovers set which now hang on the doors to the Weatherfield North tram stop ticket office. You can also find the arches from the first outdoor set within the lobby of the Factory International theatre space on Water Street which was built on the old Granada Studios site.

When Tony chatted to the press at the launch of the new studios, now named after him, he said: 'Coronation Street hasn't moved at all. It's exactly where it always was. Which is wherever you want it to be inside your own imagination.'

I just want to take you back to Lynne Carol who played Martha Longhurst. In 1964 a new young producer, Tim Aspinall, took over and he decided to kill Martha off – one of the Greek chorus of old ladies – Martha, Minnie and Ena – who held court in the Rovers' snug. Why did he do it? For publicity and ratings. On 1st April a number of the cast were informed that they had been sacked – with Lynne/Martha Longhurst to be the first one to make her exit. It was hugely shocking for the cast and Violet Carson (Ena) even threatened to resign in protest.

However, on the evening of 13th May, 1964, the nation watched Martha arrive at the Rovers where a leaving party was underway for Frank Barlow (another to be sacked). She brandished her new passport, but the regulars were busy singing songs and she retreated, feeling unwell, into the deserted Snug. She then suffered a heart attack being discovered slumped over the table by Jack and Annie Walker who fetched Len Fairclough (Peter Adamson) to check her pulse and he then declared her dead. The episode was the first to end with no theme tune – the credits rolled in silence.

The cast now knew that their careers could be sacrificed for ratings. Lynne herself, although dreadfully upset, behaved, in public at least, with decorum. She was the youngest of the three actresses – in fact when she landed the role she was just 46 playing a 64-year-old. Lynne used to relay tales of being stopped wherever she went by disgruntled fans. Some would even ask things like: 'How long have you been dead for now?' In April, 1990 Granada announced her death but it proved to be an error. She died a month later.

I have had the joy of knowing many of the cast down the years – Philip Middlemiss (Des Barnes) was a particular favourite. Phil was always a good laugh and had a lovely twinkle in his eye. Jill Summers (Phyllis Pearce) who worked with him a lot also adored him. They would often sit in the bottom end of the Green Room, when the studios were at Quay Street, which had one-way mirrored windows looking out onto the street set through the viaduct when it was open to the public and they would sit there watching the fans on the Lot. Phil would sometimes dress up in a coat and wig and go out onto the set mingling with the tourists. He would take a camera with him and stop someone saying that he was a big fan of Des Barnes and ask if they'd take his photo outside Des's house. Jill would find it hilarious. Sometimes Roy Barraclough would join in and make his way down the inside of the shells of the terrace (the houses were basically one long building) until he reached the Rovers. Fans would invariably open the pub's letterbox to see what was inside. They'd often find Alec looking back at them and telling them off for being so nosey!

Jean Alexander, who played Hilda was a lovely, gentle lady. She kindly agreed to contribute to my book on the Oldham Coliseum, I interviewed her on a couple of occasions, and I was lucky enough to be seated next to her at Liz Dawn's 60th wedding anniversary dinner. She was the polar opposite of Hilda or Auntie Wainwright, her most famous roles. She was born and brought up in Toxteth, Liverpool (named Jean Hodgkinson) the younger of two children. Her dad worked in shipbuilding and was often away for weeks at a time so when he came home, he often treated Jean and her brother Ken to a trip to the Pavilion Theatre or to shows at the seaside. This is where she became enchanted by the stage.

It was 1949 before she became a professional actress having worked as a librarian upon leaving school. That year she had left the library service and was recovering from a bad bout of pneumonia, the second in her then short life, in Barrow-in-Furness where her father was working at the time. She received a letter from a friend tipping her off that the Adelphi Guild Theatre in Macclesfield were auditioning for new cast members. She made her debut in Somerset Maugham's play *Sheppey* playing the daughter of the lead character and stayed with the company for two years – playing, she told me, an owl, Lady Macbeth and a witch amongst other roles.

A stint at Bolton, on the dole and at Oldham followed. It was here that she worked as wardrobe mistress. Jean told me that one Sunday afternoon she was in the theatre on her own and sorting through skips full of costumes when a very large, and fearless, rat jumped out and sat on the table staring at her. She was terrified – and paralysed with fear. All she could do was watch it as it strolled across the dressing room

47

table and nibbled on a stick of theatrical make-up. She told me that she decided there and then that her wardrobe days were over.

Luckily actor John Barrie, whom she had met at Oldham, told her that she was wasting her time and that she should get into television. He introduced her to agent Joan Reddin who took Jean's career in hand and remained her agent until her death. She made her first *Coronation Street* appearance in 1962 as the landlady, Mrs Webb, of the digs where Joan Akers (played by Bill Roache's first wife Anna Cropper) was staying when she kidnapped Christopher Hewitt. She returned in 1964 as Hilda Ogden alongside Bernard Youens (known as 'Bunny') as husband Stan with children Irma and Trevor. Hilda was an immensely popular character even spawning a society called The British League for Hilda Ogden which included in its membership Sir John Betjeman, Russell Harty, Sir Laurence Olivier and Michael Parkinson. Jean played Hilda until Christmas Day 1987 (when 26 million viewers tuned in to see her sing *Wish Me Luck as You Wave Me Goodbye*, in her inimitable fashion, in the Rovers) after which she joined *Last of the Summer Wine*. When she died in 2016, I was somewhat surprised to see a couple of gifts I'd given her being auctioned off. I didn't buy them back.

The first time I met Katherine Kelly she was appearing alongside Keith Clifford in his and John Chambers' play *Randle's Scandle's* about the eccentric comedian Frank Randle, described elsewhere in this book. Also appearing was Katherine's dad. The next time was when she had joined *Coronation Street* as Becky Grainger, a role she played between 2006 and 2012. Since then, of course, she's appeared in lots more TV, film and stage roles including parts in *Mr*

Selfridge, Happy Valley and *Gentleman Jack*. When she toured Canada and appeared at the British Isles Show I was engaged to interview her for the official programme.

She told me how she landed the role of Becky. 'I was asked to audition and told to go along looking scruffy. However, earlier in the day I had auditioned for something else and had been told to dress glamorously. The first audition over-ran and so I was rushing on the train to Granada, trying to take my make-up off, pull my hair about ... it was mad. I got the part straight away. It was a job for a few weeks at first - but I was kept on.'

I wondered how easy it was to play someone who, particularly when she first went into the show, was quite un-likeable. 'You don't have to like the character you play but you do have to find a reason why she is like she is,' she explained. 'The viewers watched her grow up and for me she was like seven characters in one. Bill Ward, who played Charlie Stubbs, used to say that Charlie deserved to die but that he understood how Charlie had become so evil. You must do that to play a character over a long story arc.'

Two people I met regularly were Peter Baldwin and Thelma Barlow (Derek and Mavis Wilton). Peter was a charming man who had a great passion for toy theatres, and he owned, at one time, with his brother Christopher, the famous Benjamin Pollock's Toy Shop in London's Covent Garden. Peter and Thelma worked together for the very first time in a stage production of *The Way of the World* for the West of England Theatre Company, in 1955, many years before they paired up on the cobbles. Peter made his television debut in 1969 in a comedy called *Girls About Town* but it was in 1976 whilst appearing at the King's Head Theatre in

The Browning Version that he was invited to Manchester to audition for the part of Derek Wilton.

The role was a semi-permanent part which is when a character is brought in every now and again. At first Derek would call in at The Kabin as a salesman selling stationary. An on/off relationship with Mavis (thwarted by her other beau Victor Pendlebury) played out over many years with Peter only joining the permanent cast after 12 years. Of course, Mavis and Derek decided to tie the knot – the first time they both jilted each other and then, in 1988, they became Mr and Mrs Wilton enjoying nine years together until Derek was axed by new producer Brian Park. The character suffered a heart attack in his paperclip-topped company car, and I think it fair to say that Peter never really got over it.

Thelma was born in Middlesbrough but brought up in Huddersfield following her father's death when she was just five weeks old. She worked as a secretary for eight years whilst performing with the local amateur society. She decided to turn professional and joined the Joan Littlewood Theatre Group in London. She once told me that she auditioned at the same time as Michael Caine. Contracts with several repertory companies followed ('We travelled around in an old van, putting the scenery up, learning lines for the next play on the way home – it was great experience') and it was whilst appearing in Liverpool that she auditioned for the role of Mavis Riley in 1971. Her first appearance was as a guest at Emily Nugent and Ernie Bishop's engagement party. The following year she attended their wedding, and a friendship began with builder Jerry Booth that led to her landing a job in The Kabin as Rita's assistant.

In 1997, now widowed Mavis, decided to move away and Rita agreed to join her, but things didn't work out that way and Mavis opened a guest house in Cartmel, Cumbria on her own. In reality, Thelma had informed *Coronation Street* producers that she intended to retire from the show back in 1995 and was asked to stay on for a final two years. It was this decision that would eventually lead to both Derek and Mavis leaving the show. They decided that they didn't want Derek without Mavis.

Thelma is a lovely, classy, lady who I adore. After leaving Corrie she appeared in so many wonderful roles including *Doctor Who, Mrs Henderson Presents* and *Dinnerladies.*

A cast member I didn't always see eye-to-eye with was John Savident who played butcher Fred Elliott but I have to confess that he had some fabulous stories from a wonderful career. One that he often told had him in an off license late at night around Christmas time. There was another customer in there that he half-recognised. Assuming that she must be an actress he said hello and asked whether she was working at the moment. She replied that she wasn't. 'No pantomime?' asked John. 'Oh dear!' And off he went. He was half way down the street when he realised who she was – Princess Margaret.

Someone you may not have heard of is Kevin Horkin, a great friend. Kevin has had a varied, successful, career as an entrepreneur. He used to supply animals to the show including the famous turkey which appeared in 1997. Les Battersby (Bruce Jones) 'acquired' a live turkey which he intended to fatten up for Christmas lunch. Toyah and Spider freed the bird, but it ended up being run over with the meat bearing the tyre marks. Well, Kevin supplied Teresa the Turkey to play the role. The story caught the imagination of the public and press and he enjoyed some publicity afterwards. I even had Teresa come to the Oldham Coliseum Theatre, where we mocked up a picture of her 'holding' a copy of the play *Much Ado About Stuffing* saying she was moving on from soap and hoping to train as a serious actress. She certainly got her ten minutes of fame.

Another friend who owned a few of the Corrie animals was location manager Anne Wilkie-Miller (christened 'Anne Milky-Coffee' by Kevin Kennedy). Anne, and her husband Tony, had spent their careers in television and were wonderful people. When Anne retired from Corrie they opened a guest house in Abersoch, North Wales. There they lived with Scamper, who played the dog of the same name belonging to Judy Mallet's mother, Percy's budgie Randy and Mavis's budgie Harriet. It was like Sunset Boulevard for animals. Anne worked on the regular show, but she also worked on the QE2 special. The whole thing (you might recall it covered Raquel and Curly's honeymoon) was filmed during a real voyage on the QE2, all except one sequence where Rita and Alec stand on the back of the ship and look out to sea. Fireworks explode in the night sky. Well, that couldn't be filmed at sea as the fireworks would have been taken as distress signals so that scene had to be shot in a field in Cheshire. A quick side tale – the passengers who were booked on the QE2 voyage that the Corrie crew would be on board for weren't told in advance. It was all hush-hush. Two of those passengers, who'd been looking forward to a couple of weeks away from work, were Betty Driver and her sister. And one of the guest speakers was Tony Warren!

Another mate is Jennie McAlpine (Fiz). Again, I first met her when I was sent to interview her ahead of her Canadian appearance back in 2008. Jennie is from Bury and joined Corrie at the age of 17. She was brought up by her dad Tom who I also had the pleasure of getting to know. 'It was he who introduced me to theatre,' she told me. 'I played the fairy, and he played the Dame in the local amateur theatre pantomime when I was young – and that was the spark.' She then started doing stand-up comedy making the finals of the Comedian of the Year two years running, aged just 13 and 14. 'We had to perform at the Comedy Store in London – I think I was/am the youngest person to perform there!'

She then joined the theatre workshop in her home town alongside Vicky Binns and Nikki Sanderson. After college she began auditioning for professional roles and appeared in *Emmerdale* before crossing the Pennines and landing in Weatherfield. She is married to Chris Farr and together they have three children, and they own a popular restaurant in Manchester city centre. In fact, when they first started going out together Jennie and I were due to go on a publicity trip to Canada. Chris had asked her out on another date, and she told him that she couldn't – she was going to Canada with another man. That was me.

Maggie Jones not only played Deirdre's mother Blanche to perfection – she also looked as you'd imagine Anne Kirkbride's mother to look. Maggie joined the show in 1974 taking over the role after the death of Patricia Cutts who first played Blanche. Maggie had appeared in a whole range of roles before arriving permanently on the cobbles in 1999 – everything from *The Forsyte Saga, In Sickness and In Health, Sharon and Elsie* and *Heartbeat.* I always think of her when I go to the Victoria and Albert Hotel in Manchester. It's where she usually stayed when filming Corrie when the studios were across the road. She had a favourite seat in the bar and could usually be found there, studying her scripts.

I regularly took Corrie fan groups there for dinner and I'd be sure to arrive early so that I could check whether Maggie was in her usual place by the door to the restaurant. 'Oh, dearheart, you're here again!' she'd say before we'd turn her chair around so that she wouldn't be disturbed. She would then make sure that she was visible when the group was leaving so that she could say goodbye to everyone before making her way up to her room. Blanche was of course known for her acerbic remarks like telling Ken and Deirdre that good looks were a curse so they should count themselves lucky. Maggie had a sharp sense of humour herself and was always up for a natter. Looking across the bar she made a comment about a young couple who couldn't keep their hands off each other. 'Look at those two – isn't that what a bus shelter's for?'

I can't remember the first time I met Barbara Knox, but it was about three decades ago and she quickly became a close friend. We have enjoyed many an evening out – dinners, the theatre, and a few fan events. She is kind, funny and adores the theatre. One evening Roy, Barbara and I were dining at the Midland Hotel. They both mentioned that the couple at the next table were continually glancing at them, but they didn't know who they were. I turned around to find David and Victoria Beckham smiling in our direction. I wonder what happened to the two of them.

Barbara appeared in *A Family at War, Emergency Ward 10, Never Mind the Quality Feel the Width* and *George and the Dragon* amongst other shows, but it was whilst appearing with Ken Dodd in his series that she was asked to join *Coronation Street* as a regular. She was under contract to do a whole series with Ken so she had to go to him and ask if she could leave the show – he agreed, which many performers wouldn't have done.

Roy avoided going to awards events if he could – they are often very long and quite boring but when, in 2004, Barbara was to be given the British Soap Award's Lifetime Achievement award Roy agreed to present it to her and we both went to BBC Television Centre for the recording. It was something he was very honoured to do – for a life-long friend.

Barbara and I still enjoy a natter. And a sing-song.

Sue Nicholls is the daughter of Lord Harmer Nicholls and is therefore The Right Honourable Susan Nicolls. She has appeared in so many wonderful productions – *Rentaghost, The Rise and Fall of Reginald Perrin, Pipkins, Crossroads* and *Coronation Street*. She's appeared on Broadway and she's even had a song in the charts. In 1993 she married Mark Eden who played Alan Bradley.

Sue is a very funny lady and has the most infectious laugh. She often performs potted versions of musicals – and she does it brilliantly. She's also absolutely lovely.

William Roache is also a lovely man. As everyone knows he has played Ken Barlow since Corrie's first episode back in 1960. When he was a member of Oldham Rep for a short period, which is mentioned elsewhere in this book, he was dating actress Anna Cropper, who was also working there. It was noted at a board meeting that Bill's hair was too long and that he should get it cut – and that he was seeing Miss Cropper – and that they should marry. He did both.

Bill is just the type of person you need as a company leader really – he is kind, caring, relaxed and utterly professional. I have worked with him quite a few times – interviewing him at fan events, hosting Christmas light-switch on's with him and, I'm very honoured to say, writing a notable speech for him – the one he delivered at Manchester Pride in 2023. Whenever I meet him we always fall into discussions about the old days and about the actors who used to inhabit the studios.

Vicky Entwistle is one of the funniest people I know. I'm just not sure she knows how funny she is. She is also the best audience you could possibly wish for. I adore her. She is also nothing like Janice Battersby. She, Bruce Jones, Jane Danson and Georgia Taylor had a baptism of fire when they arrived on the cobbles as the loud-mouthed Battersby's back in 1997. They were described by the press office as 'Weatherfield's answer to Wayne and Waynetta Slob' and were brought in to shake things up. They certainly did. Vick left the show in 2011 and since then has appeared in plays and pantomimes and has shown that there's certainly life after Corrie.

Meg Johnson, who died in 2023, was another favourite of mine. Meg played Eunice Gee in Corrie, Brigid McKenna in *Brookside* and Pearl Ladderbanks in *Emmerdale*. Meg (or Margaret Mary as I called her – her full name) made her stage debut in Bolton whilst evacuated from her home in Manchester. She was a keen singer (she found it helped her breathing and relieved her asthma) and appeared with lots of amateur operatic societies. In 1960 she was asked to appear at Oldham Rep (Oldham Coliseum) with the professional company – an association that lasted four decades. She once told me that she was in the nursing home having given birth to her first child, Nicholas, when the offer came. She was so nervous of telling the nursing sister that she was returning to work so soon – and worse, planning to take her baby with her – that she put it off until the last minute. 'We were given a dressing room on the ground floor so that Nicholas could come onto the stage in his pram and any actor who didn't have lines took it in turns to rock him. He didn't come to any harm!' she told me.

She appeared in dozens of West End shows including *Oliver!, Follies, Carousel, Annie Get Your Gun, Chicago* and *42nd Street*. As well as her musical and soap appearances she is probably best remembered for her work with Victoria Wood. Meg had various 'normal' jobs in the early days including a stint as a dental receptionist. Her first husband was a dentist, Hibbert Johnson, and her second husband was the equally lovely Charles Foster, actor and TV continuity announcer.

Both Meg and Charles appeared at the Oldham Coliseum a few times during my stint there. Charles in *The Cemetery Club* and *Underneath the Arches* and Meg in a host of plays and musicals from *Saturday Night at the Crown* to *Loadsamoney*. She would often arrive at the theatre in a hurry – something having gone wrong en route – and having abandoned the car in a full car park. More than once I'd have to move her car or try and get a parking ticket rescinded!

FOUR – ROY, THE REP & CANADA

Roy Barraclough was born in Preston, an only child. His father, Philip, was a part-time professional football player and full-time stonemason. His mum, Florence, worked for her family's ice cream business. His parents were keen theatregoers and at the age of 10 he was taken to see a production of *The Desert Song* at the Preston Royal Hippodrome. In the interval he managed to sneak backstage and was in awe of this glimpse into another world. It fired his imagination and the next day he made himself a puppet theatre from a cardboard box, the first of many over the years - and as they got more elaborate, so he experimented with scenic effects and lighting – on several occasions fusing the lights in his parent's home.

Regular trips to plays, pantomimes and variety shows followed and at the age of 14 he had saved up enough pocket money to buy himself a season ticket for the weekly repertory theatre. Watching a different play each week from his seat in the 4th row of the circle and seeing such people as Frederick Jaegar, Jean Kent, Derek Benfield and Leonard Rossiter.

He then joined Preston Drama Club and quickly built a reputation as a talented amateur actor often appearing alongside a young Susan Hanson (later Miss Diane in *Crossroads*) and Mavis Rogerson (later Edna Gee in *Coronation Street*). At the age of 16 he was employed to play a schoolboy in a production of *The Housemaster* starring John Barron (later CJ in the Reggie Perrin series). It was his first professional engagement, and he was paid £4 for the week. He now began to dream of a career in the theatre.

His dad wasn't convinced, and so Roy enrolled at Preston's Harris Technical College and later joined the engineering works of Thomas A. Blackburn as a draughtsman. He hated every minute of it and spent as much time as he could acting, writing, directing, designing scenery and costumes – and playing the piano - for countless amateur shows.

Apart from a couple of pantomime appearances, one with variety star Albert Modley, a troupe of performing poodles and a monkey called Jacko, and a short stint as a comic and pianist in a holiday camp on the Isle of Wight he was still plugging away at the unfulfilling day job, albeit for the decent salary of £26 a week. But in 1962 he managed to escape when he was offered a contract at the Huddersfield Repertory Company. It might have been his dream job, but it also meant a huge drop in pay, leaving home and abandoning a trade for the most precarious of careers.

Eventually he moved on to Stoke's Theatre-in-the-Round working alongside Robert Powell and Ben Kingsley – and he joined Oldham Repertory Theatre in 1966. Every week a different play – performing one at night and rehearsing another during the day. Working with the same company of actors but playing a huge range of roles. Many of the company members would feature in his life beyond Oldham – Pat Phoenix, Lynne Carol, Julie Goodyear, Jean Fergusson, Barbara Knox, Anne Kirkbride, John Jardine, Peter Dudley, Meg Johnson, Dora Bryan and so many more.

Roy's favourite playwright was Arthur Miller and he appeared in many of his plays. In years to come he would prove to be a celebrated Willy Loman, the world-worn salesman in the classic play *Death of a Salesman* but he first played the part in Oldham whilst in his early 30's, far too young for it. He recalled being on stage one Saturday matinee thinking he was perhaps getting away with it. That is until, during a long solo speech, he heard a voice in the stalls saying to her friend: 'I prefer it when they're all on, don't you?'

At one time Roy held the record for playing more characters in *Coronation Street* than any other actor starting in 1965 as a tour guide taking Annie Walker, Ena Sharples, the Ogdens and the Tanners amongst others on a tour of some Derbyshire caves in a boat (he was terrified he'd tip the boat over and never work in TV again despite the fact that the underground lake was built as a set in the studio and therefore the water wasn't that deep) then a bed salesman, a guitar salesman, Rita's agent and of course, Alec Gilroy who appeared first in 1972.

In 1986 he re-appeared as Alec on a short-term contract. In the story the Rovers had caught fire (thanks to Jack Duckworth's dodgy electrical work) and was closed so Alec was bought in to run the Graffiti Club across the road. Then Julie Goodyear's mother, Alice, was taken ill and she temporarily left the show to care for her so Roy was put into the Rovers itself and the storyline had Bet run away. Sadly, Julie's mother died and when she was able to return to work the story had Alec going to Spain to find her and proposing marriage. The proposal itself was filmed at a hotel in Mijas near Malaga and the bar scenes in Torremolinos. One evening after filming Roy and Julie were having dinner near the beach when out of the sea came a group of men with candles carrying a statue of the Virgin Mary. 'Oh,' cried Julie. 'Look, it's Alice, my mother, sending a message!' Julie often saw signs and messages in things. 'Don't be so bloody daft,' replied Roy. 'They do it every Tuesday.' And they both dissolved into laughter. It had broken the ice between them.

Both Roy and Julie were a little concerned when they were told that Bet and Alec were to marry – both characters were larger than life and somewhat mismatched - and they weren't sure whether it would work on screen. Neither did many of Bet's ardent fans. On the day of the filming of the wedding at Prestolee Church in Bolton a large crowd had gathered who chanted 'Don't do it!' Bet's wedding dress was enormous and, according to Roy, nuns had gone blind sewing sequins on it through endless nights. It really was spectacular - leg of mutton sleeves, huge crinoline. If she'd have fallen from a bridge she'd have parachuted to safety. But so much time and effort had gone into the frock that they'd forgotten to give Alec's suit much attention and the trousers were way too long – the only solution on offer was a large roll of sellotape so he had the indignity of having to have tape wrapped round his ankles in front of the rest of the cast and crew.

Both Roy and Julie always knew their lines, always went to great lengths to try and make the Rovers set as realistic as possible, poured all the drinks and even tried to give the right change. But they could both be mischievous. Alec was often seen in the back of shot with a knife up the backside of the Sooty charity collecting tin which sat on the bar, or he and Bill Tarmey would improvise some business with Jack's watch, banging it on the bar top or taking it to pieces. They must have done that dozens of times. Many an actor has told a tale of Roy making them laugh on a take or causing them to eat too much or drink too much and having difficulty saying their lines.

Lynne Perrie (Ivy Tilsley) used to tell a yarn about filming barmaid Tina Fowler's leaving do. She had been in Dawn Acton's dressing room and hadn't heard the tannoy call to go to the studio floor. Anyway, they had already begun filming the scene when she was finally located so she had to sneak onto the Rovers set mid-scene and hope that she wasn't spotted. Trying to blend in she found a space between some extras and grabbed a sausage roll off a plate on the bar which she held as if thinking about eating it. Things kept going wrong – someone missed a line, there was a problem with lighting and so on. Once an actor has a prop in their hand, they have to keep it there for continuity so Lynne ended up gripping that sausage roll so long that under the hot lights it started to disintegrate and go limp. Roy urged her to put the remnants back on the plate but she daren't in case someone else picked it up. 'It was rancid by now,' she said. On the next take she decided to eat the thing whole and pushed it into her mouth only to find that this was the precise moment she had a line. Vera turned to her, gave her the cue line and Lynne spat it all out in front of Liz Dawn, who was aghast. Roy passed Lynne a glass of water which she quickly swigged but by now was laughing so much that she spat that down Vera's dress as well. Liz Dawn (Vera) couldn't believe what she was seeing. Lynne got told off – for being late and ruining the take.

Famously Bill Waddington (Percy) had difficulty remembering his script. When Roy started working in the Rovers, he used to go on set before anyone else, to practice pouring the drinks and timing how long he had to walk from the bar to the till or how long it would take to pour a round so that he could do it and be back in place for his next line. Arriving early one day he cleared away all the cardboard Newton and Ridley drinks mats on the bar. When they started filming Percy had to come in, order, and then had a bit of chatty dialogue with Alec. Action! In came Bill who walked to the bar and then looked befuddled. 'Who's moved me script?' he muttered. He'd also been on set early and had written all his lines on beer mats which he'd carefully spread out along the bar – the ones Roy had moved. Bill sometimes wrote lines inside his cap with a marker pen but because it is very hot on set thanks to the lighting when he removed his hat, he'd sometimes have the words printed back to front on his forehead.

Bill Tarmey and Liz Dawn (Jack and Vera) also sometimes struggled with the scripts and in some of their scenes if you look carefully you'll see that spread in front of them is an array of sauce bottles, racing papers etc – all there to hide the lines. Nigel Pivaro (Terry) once told me that when he did scenes with Liz, she would often be making the Duckworth's tea and she would lift up various saucepan lids as she talked – of course, she had her lines carefully written inside each one.

Bill and Liz were both lovely. Bill and his wife Ali lived fairly close by, and we had many a meal together and I sometimes went to listen to him singing in the concert room of his local pub, the Broadoak. Liz and her husband Don shared a car with us several times going to events. Liz Dawn didn't know how naturally funny she was. She would often say things and you'd laugh, and she'd give a quizzical look not knowing, I think, why you were laughing and whether it was with or against her. It was always with. She had funny bones.

Not long after I left London for Manchester I saw a job advertised in the marketing department at the Oldham Coliseum Theatre. When I turned up for the interview there was Kenneth Alan Taylor – one of three interviewers. Kenneth explained to the other panellists that we knew each other and recused himself from the process. I got the job. I got the good news on the Thursday and started at the Coliseum on the Monday. Perhaps I only got the job because I could start quickly as the person I was replacing had already left. My first day was also the first day of the pantomime rehearsals so it was a hectic start – and there was also a note in the desk diary along the lines of 'BBC coming to follow you for fly-on-the-wall documentary'.

At 11 o'clock said BBC interviewer/producer arrived with a hearty 'Hiya Chuck!' She was like a human firework, she positively fizzed. Jane Hodson came into my life, and she's been a close and very dear friend and colleague ever since. As she often says she's my 'media wife' but I'll come back to that. Jane worked for BBC Radio Manchester (or as it was called in those days, GMR) and she followed me and the theatre company around for several weeks making a radio documentary called *It's Behind You!* lifting the lid on the staging of a regional pantomime. It was nominated for a prestigious Sony award too!

During my time at the Coliseum, we had a lot of laughs, and a few tears. The marketing department is of course responsible for the theatre's profile and for ensuring that the tickets sell but we also looked after, for some reason, bars and catering, front of house and box office, cleaning and car parking. The joys of a regional theatre. I also, under Ken's guidance, booked visiting productions, read submitted scripts and gave my views on casting. We were probably the last of the actor-managed theatres and we were a real team. Ken directed lots of the shows, appeared in some, cast as many local actors as he could, and ruled over the empire as a (sometimes) benign dictator. Occasionally the Arts Council or some funder or other would metaphorically punch us and the boat would rock a bit but by and large we did what we thought was right. And you know what? We sold over 90% of the available tickets most years.

One of my main roles was to oversee the publicity, particularly the press coverage. In those days we didn't have to bother about social media, it was down to getting articles in the local press, on radio and if possible, and it wasn't often so, on regional TV. In Oldham at the time we had two newspapers – *The Oldham Chronicle* which came out each weekday and the *Advertiser*, a free weekly. Both would attend photo-calls and interview opportunities and there was a bit of friendly rivalry between them. As a general rule I would set up a photo opportunity for the first day of rehearsal, run interviews during the three-week rehearsal period, invite the press along to do a photo on the set on the day of the dress rehearsal and then the reviewers would come along on the opening night. If tickets sales were sluggish after that then I'd try and dream something up. I remember one of the editors telling me that if someone wanted something in the newspaper then he considered that advertising. If they didn't then it was news. I tried to straddle that line.

As a rule, actors don't enjoy giving interviews so that could be an issue. Some would do anything to avoid speaking to the press, but they all recognised the need to generate publicity so would give in reluctantly if they had to. I would offer to sit in on the interviews and mostly the actor would agree. This meant that I could step in (if it was newspaper) and answer a question, steer the actor in the right direction or stop a question that I knew the actor wouldn't like. For radio the actor was on their own. I would take them to the studio (briefing them and sometimes planting possible answers) in the car. I would then sit with the producer looking at my poor actor being interviewed, through a thick pane of glass. Actors tend, privately, to be quite shy and interviews are akin to eating razorblades. I think that shyness gives them an acute understanding of the importance of communication – and a unique sensitivity. It's perhaps what they need to do their job.

Malcolm Hebden (Corrie's Norris) directed a few plays for us. The first one was a comedy set in New York called *The Cemetery Club* about a group of widows who meet up each week in the cemetery where their husbands are buried. I managed to get permission from Granada TV to allow us to do the first day rehearsal photos on the New York set of the old studio tours. It made a fabulous, colourful setting. Advance ticket sales weren't good, and I was concerned that the title of the play was putting people off – it sounded depressing - so when it came to the dress rehearsal photo I shared my concerns with Malcolm. The set revolved and on one side was the cemetery set with gravestones and a grey bench and on the other was a jazzy New York apartment. I told Malcolm that I only wanted to use the apartment set and that we should keep the cemetery set hidden. He agreed.

When the press photographers arrived, we ushered them into the auditorium, and we introduced the cast and the apartment set and explained the story and how funny it was. 'Oh,' said one photographer to Malcolm, 'I thought it'd be about death.' Malcolm told him that I was worried that if we let them photograph the cemetery set it'd put people off. With that he instructed the backstage team to revolve the set to show the photographer what they couldn't use. Of course, that's all they'd photograph so my plan backfired.

The longer I worked there the more fascinated I became with the theatre's history and I loved reading through the archives of press cuttings and programmes, at least the ones we had. My colleague Sue Evans and I started to look for more – we made some appeals and slowly we started to put together a fuller archive. Sue also spent a lot of time building up lists of actors and plays and so on. I was sitting in on an interview with one of our actors and a magazine journalist one day and as I walked the journalist out he asked me about the building and its past. I gave him a quick tour reciting some of the stories about it that I'd picked up. He told me that he owned the magazine and that he also published books and if ever I wanted to write one on the theatre to let him know.

A few weeks later I did just that. Peter Riley, sadly no longer with us, published what became *They Started Here!* which was a history of the theatre with recollections from various actors who had graced its stage. People including Dame Sian Phillips, Jean Alexander, Roy, Barbara Knox, Bill Roache, Meg Johnson and Dora Bryan. There were some great stories – Bill told of making his debut in pantomime as *Robin Hood* and feeling very glam and matinee idol-ish. His first entrance was a walk down a big staircase with the children of the chorus lining it shouting, 'Here comes Robin!' Unfortunately, on the first night he slipped and fell all the way down, landing on his backside.

My dear friend John Jardine told of playing an ugly sister opposite Paula Tilbrook in *Cinderella*. One day the stage management went to get the real ponies and carriage ready for Cinders' transformation into the ball gown. They realised that the ponies had eaten all the tinsel and decorations off the carriage but there wasn't time to do anything about it. Cinderella had to climb aboard a pretty threadbare coach and as the spotlight lit her up so one of the ponies did a huge poo right in the middle of the stage. John swore that it glittered in the lights.

When the book came out, we had a launch party at the theatre and so many of my friends came along – John Stevenson, John Jardine, Paula Tilbrook, Meg Johnson, Charles Foster, Eric Potts, Alan Rothwell, Lynette McMorrough, Kenneth Alan Taylor and many more. It was a lovely 'do' until I was asked to say a few words and then, for the only time in my adult life, I just couldn't speak. I was so overcome by the months of work producing a book I was proud of, and which people wanted to buy – and by all the support I had - that I could only string a few words together.

The book did really well and Roy, John Jardine and I even did a book signing aboard the Arcadia cruise ship – and they sold out of stock! Dora Bryan wrote a lovely letter to the *Oldham Chronicle* praising the book and saying that she had had five years of training at the theatre 'that cannot be taught or bought.' One story Dora shared was when she was Stage Manager for a production of Ibsen's *The Ghosts* – a heavy Norwegian tragedy. At the Saturday matinee the director announced that he was going into Manchester so Dora took the opportunity to 'cheer things up' by, instead of playing a recording of classical music during the interval, playing Joe Loss's *In the*

Mood. Unfortunately, the director hadn't made it into Manchester due to fog so heard the swap. Dora was sacked then re-instated. Not, I understand, for the first, or last, time.

The book led to lots of opportunities – I started to be asked to be a 'talking head' (that's when you pontificate about things) on radio and TV about pantomime, variety theatre and Oldham. Some of the requests were a bit odd – the BBC rang one day asking if I would talk on the radio about Oldham's aeroplane building history. I replied that I knew very little, if anything, about it. 'Well, I can't get anyone else and you did a book about Oldham so ...' said the researcher hopefully. About Oldham's theatre - not its industry. Occasionally we'd be asked to help with research for a TV show. The most common was *This Is Your Life* whose researchers would often ring up and swear you to secrecy before asking questions about some actor or other. I was always slightly guarded because Roy had hated his appearance on the show – more of which in a later chapter.

I did quite a lot of research for Anne Kirkbride's tribute (codenamed by the producers 'Free' inspired by Deirdre's stint behind bars) and the other one was Paula Tilbrook's (codenamed 'Gossip'). I suggested they talk to John Jardine about her because he knew her really well and had worked with her many times – they booked him to come through the famous doors – and he told that tale about the panto ponies as only John could - hilariously. I was asked if I would sit on stage for the show even though, at that point, I'd never actually met Paula. I was instructed to arrive about three hours before the recording at the Manchester BBC Studios, then in Oxford Road. I declined to do so. When they insisted, I told them to forget it, but they eventually agreed to let me do my own make-up at home and arrive half an hour before. They must have desperately needed one more man to make up the numbers!

I mentioned the lovely Alan Rothwell earlier. I was always a bit in awe of Alan actually but not a gentler man could you wish to meet. I grew up watching him presenting *Picture Box* on a big TV which was wheeled into the school hall. To others he will be forever remembered as Ken's brother David Barlow in *Corrie*, or Nicholas Black in *Brookside* or maybe for *Hickory House* or *Emmerdale* – he's done it all. Well Alan directed and appeared in many Coliseum productions. One Saturday he and Roy had been asked to attend a fete at a local hospital. Roy and I turned up and there was a gazebo with a table and two chairs set under it for them both to sit at. Alan didn't arrive so I sat in his chair whilst a queue of people made donations to chat to Roy. Alan never did turn up but after an hour I saw a chap wearing a pair of big headphones and talking into a microphone hove into view. He was patently on air. Then I heard him say: 'And here are two of the most recognisable faces on TV today – Roy Barraclough and Alan Rothwell. Hello Alan!'

I looked around thinking Alan must have arrived - but no. He was talking to me. 'Everyone will know you for your days in *Coronation Street* Alan. Tell us about that!' Then the microphone was pushed in front of me. I didn't want to embarrass the presenter but what could I say? 'I'm not Alan,' I said quietly not really wanting the listeners to hear. 'Great – what was it like working with Bill Roache?' and so it went on. To each of the half dozen or so questions I replied that I wasn't Alan. Not a flicker. He ploughed on with the interview. And then, pleased with himself, interviewed Roy. So, just for the record, I am NOT Alan Rothwell.

I also got asked to give talks at local groups – the WI, Rotary, Probus and people like that. I started doing so and over the years I've expanded the repertoire and still enjoy public speaking to this day. One of the talks I give is about the history of *Coronation Street* – and that started thanks to the book also. I was at the Coliseum when I got a call from someone in the Corrie production office – would I be able to give a guided tour of the theatre to a group of Canadian *Coronation Street* fans who were over on a sort of pilgrimage holiday? Yes! So, the date and time was set, and Roy, Alan Rothwell and Kenneth Alan Taylor all agreed to come along too. Now, I knew something of these Canadian holidays because a friend of ours, Roy Power, who provided the cars which drove the Corrie cast to location filming, had been involved with them for years and he'd booked both Roy and I to meet groups in the past.

On the appointed day the group arrived by coach with their British guide Ailsa (who it later turned out was Paula Tilbrook's cousin and had been sat in front of me on her *This Is Your Life* – a small world!) and we put on a very popular tour and autograph session. If I remember correctly the following year, they went to see Roy and Chloe Newsome *(Corrie's* Vicky) in *Spring and Port Wine* at the West Yorkshire Playhouse. Anyway, at some point I was asked whether I would be interested in taking over as tour guide for the full 10 days as Ailsa wasn't well. I said yes, the theatre released me for a fortnight as it coincided with our summer break, and I read up as much about Corrie as I could.

The holidays include visits to filming locations – the church, the courts and so on, a tour of the studios, a few outings to places such as Blackpool and the Peak District and meals with various cast members who I sometimes interview. It's always very tiring but I love seeing their reactions when they go onto the street lot for the first time or come face-to-face with a legend such as Barbara Knox or David Neilson – and it's fun to see the place I live in with visitors and to see their reactions to things we take for granted. It's quite a privilege. I did it for about twenty years when I decided I'd hand it on to someone else. That didn't quite work out and as I write this I'm back in as the 'man with the microphone' if only for a year or two. It keeps drawing me back.

A little diversion – the real vicar of the church where they shoot most of the wedding and funeral scenes told me a lovely story. In 2003 there was a storyline where, at a church fundraiser, Rita, Emily, Roy, Norris and the vicar got spaced out after inadvertently eating hash brownies served up by Vera. A few months later Eileen Derbyshire (Emily) was at the church filming something else when she encountered the real vicar showing around a couple who were thinking of getting married there. The vicar acknowledged Eileen who looked at him and laughingly said: 'Not getting high on the cannabis today!' Of course, this was the real vicar – the one who'd been 'high' was an actor. The bridal couple must have wondered what was going on!

Roy left Corrie for the last time in the autumn of 1998 and in early 1999 we went to Canada on a publicity tour which coincided with his on-screen departure being aired there.

We were based in Toronto and for four days Roy would be making appearances at the *British Isles Show* which was a large fair open to the public promoting British products. Ronnie Corbett was there selling *Two Ronnies* DVD's, there were two Page Three girls flogging calendars and Roy promoting Corrie. He had a big backdrop of the street behind him, a chap dressed up as a British policeman keeping the lines in order and his own photographer. Nearby was parked a large motorhome which we used as our rest area. Literally thousands of Canadian Corrie fans queued each day to meet him, have a photo taken and get a signed picture.

One day I asked if it was possible for us to be taken into town for lunch rather than have a sandwich in the motorhome. It was all set up and we were driven to a so-called British pub. As the car pulled up outside a crowd of onlookers stopped and cheered. Then we noticed a sign reading 'Come and watch Alex (sic) Gilroy have his lunch!' We sat at our table as if on stage, dozens of eyes watching every move and flash bulbs going off continually. We ate in the motorhome every day after that.

There were other functions and press things to do and it was very tiring. At one, after a long day, the British High Commissioner was in attendance. He sympathised with Roy's tiredness and slipped us out by a back door arranging to have us driven back to our hotel in his official car. I don't know how long it was before they realised the guest of honour had gone - if they ever did. The day after the show finished, we and the Page Three girls were taken to Niagara to see the famous falls although as it was March and minus 18 so they were somewhat frozen – as were we. After that, for a few years at least, I became a regular visitor to the show often accompanying a cast member.

One year I was asked by the organisers of the British Isles Show if I could take a look-a-like with me who would represent Britain. The year before I had directed two shows at the now closed Tameside Hippodrome marking the Queen's 80th birthday and then, the jubilee. The acts included Jimmy Cricket, Jean Fergusson (as Hylda Baker), Kathy Staff, Roy, a fabulous ventriloquist called Neville King (he told me a lovely tale of appearing at a working men's club – the secretary told him after the first house that the act would be improved if the dummy stood closer to the microphone – he'd be heard better!) and a very convincing Prince William look-a-like called Matthew Turpin. Matthew agreed to come to Canada with us. He was such a lovely young chap who had put himself through university and was now a financial analyst. He took his royal job very seriously but was relaxed off-duty and great company. Anyway, I flew over to Toronto with him and as the 'plane approached the pilot made the following announcement: 'The snow is bad in Toronto, so we won't be able to land right now. We're being diverted to Ottawa and hopefully we have enough fuel to make it.' Matthew and I looked at each other hoping the pilot simply had a dark sense of humour. Well, we did make it to Ottawa and we did re-fuel and after a short while being kept aboard the stationary aircraft we set off again and this time managed to land in Toronto. The runway was being cleared and snow was piled high everywhere. I've never seen anything like it.

We made our way through customs with Matthew attracting some attention because of who he resembled. Through baggage reclaim, and then we found out that there was no public transport and no taxis. We were rescued by the people from the British Isles Show who arranged with someone else for a sort of jeep-like vehicle to take us to Mississauga, the city which neighbours Toronto where we were put up for the night and treated rather royally before being conveyed to our hotel the next morning. I never did find out if the home's owners thought they had had Prince William and his equerry to stay. Better not to ask.

On another occasion Shobna Gulati, who played Sunita, was the guest at the show and I was travelling over on my own to catch up with Canadian friends and attend some *Corrie* quiz nights. I was asked by the studios if I would take a raffle prize with me – it was the prop wedding album from Sunita's marriage to Dev. This large red leather book contained lots of pictures from the filming of the wedding episode including Dev arriving on horseback at the Hindu Temple (actually the old Granada Breeze studio at the Quay Street studios).

When I arrived at Toronto customs, I got routinely stopped but I knew I had nothing on me that I shouldn't. However, when they found the wedding album it started a lot of questions. Why did I have an Asian family's wedding album? Why wasn't I in any of the pictures? I asked the slightly stern officer whether they watched *Coronation Street*. They didn't. A supervisor was called. Luckily, he did. He asked if he could take a picture with the album to show his wife and off I went. Thankfully.

Each year, as I've said, I look after groups of Canadian Corrie fans coming to the UK. It's hard work but great fun. It starts about nine months in advance when I put together an itinerary for each day working out where to go, how long it will take the coach to get between the stops, where we'll eat and so on. I plot the routes out literally street by street so that we pass filming locations or places associated with the show. On the face of it that could be -stopping at a church, driving past a supermarket, calling at a pub for lunch and then posing for pictures by the side of a canal. It isn't where we go so much as the memories I hope to convey when we're there so yes, it could look an ordinary canal but when you start talking about how it was used to film Richard Hillman's kidnapping of the Platt family and driving in to the icy waters, how it was filmed, how the stunts were performed and so on … well, it's my job to make it live I suppose.

The tours have meant that I've been asked over the years, often by Granada, to appear on various other TV shows including a documentary on the life of the legendary Irish actor Ray McAnally presented by his son Aonghus. We spent a Sunday afternoon filming around the Granada studios on Quay Street talking about what life would have been like there when his dad had worked on *The Fellows* and *Crown Court*. It was a very pleasant job and we filmed on the site of the old New York lot and on Grape Street which led to the *Coronation Street* set. Aonghus was curious to see the Corrie set so we moved crab-like towards it only to be stopped by a security guard who shouted, 'I don't care who you are – you're not going on there!' Charming!

Amongst the other TV appearances as a 'talking head' was *Mystery Hunters* for Discovery. They sent a Canadian crew over with presenter Araya Mengesha to film at the Coliseum and have me talk about the theatre's ghost. In 1947 during a performance of 'The Scottish Play' (it's unlucky to say *Macbeth* but hopefully not to write it) the sword fight went wrong and poor actor Harold Norman was stabbed. He died some days later from peritonitis at the local hospital. Bernard Cribbins appeared in the show, but he was also looking after the props. He was only nineteen or thereabouts. Many accounts say that the sword's safety tip came off but Bernard told me that there never was a safety tip – real swords were used. Well, Harold's ghost is said to haunt the theatre and there have been many reported sightings – including my own. Theatres are spooky places in the dark but one afternoon I entered the circle from one side of the building and crossed the darkened and empty auditorium to get to my office on the other side. About three quarters of the way across I felt a shove, but no one was there. Was that Harold? Who knows - but I have acted it out on TV more than once over the years.

For some time, before moving north, I was a volunteer tour guide at London's Highgate Cemetery and in that capacity, I appeared on a number of shows including with Alan Titchmarsh on *Pebble Mill at One* and also on Danny Baker's BBC show and most unusually, on the Chinese equivalent of *Wish You Were Here*, the travel show. The crew and presenters were very formal and at the end I was presented, with great ceremony and lots of bowing, with a government-issue tie in a plastic sleeve. When I tried to wear it I discovered that it was like cardboard and couldn't possibly be worn!

I've appeared on shows such as *BBC Breakfast* and *Granada Tonight* talking about various aspects of *Coronation Street* and I appeared in a Canadian documentary called *Corrie Crazy* presented by Debbie Travis, an English-born Canadian TV host and design guru. She, and a sizeable crew, came over to the UK to film the show which largely looked at how popular it was in Canada – and why. My first scene was at Portland Basin, the canal where Richard Hillman drove into the water, and concluded at the park in Salford which doubles as the famous Red Rec in the series. Debbie was great fun and we hit it off straight away. The show was aired for *Coronation Street's* 50th birthday and brought me a great deal of publicity and recognition amongst the Canadian fan base.

I did a couple of interviews for overseas shows with Tony Warren, Corrie's creator. Tony didn't like talking about the show – well, it must have been boring, mustn't it? The first time I had been asked to arrive at the hotel where the filming was taking place quite early, an hour before I was due in front of the camera. They always do this and often make a great fuss about hair and make-up. Well, I have no hair and usually slap a bit of 'de-shine' on my bald head to stop it glinting under the lights before I leave home. (These days I also paint the eyebrows in with a bit of black too – but that's getting older for you! As my grandmother used to say, 'Old age never comes alone!' – for me it comes with an eyebrow pencil!). Anyhow, I duly arrived only to find Tony having a cigarette outside. He didn't really want to do the interview, he wasn't in the mood, but he was due in front of the cameras before me. Off I went to find the make-up lady leaving Tony outside. Well, he only went and left! So, they made me do his bit too. I loved chatting with him. He was so clever, so great a storyteller – and so funny.

One of the best things was when I just had to sit there and say nothing. In 2000 the BBC announced that they were starting a Hall of Fame at Broadcasting House and they'd be inducting various people into this 'hall' which would form part of an exhibition open to the public. The first person was Barbara Windsor and Roy and I were asked to be part of the celebrity audience for the TV show. I think, I may be wrong, but I think they only did Barbara's and then gave it up as a bad lot. Whatever, we went – and Roy filmed a sketch with Christopher Biggins as two guards at the BBC patrolling this 'Hall of Fame'. The show, hosted by Dale Winton, was recorded at Wembley and we sat at a table with Fern Britton and her then husband Phil Vickery.

Other people there included John Inman, Una Stubbs, Danny La Rue, Amanda Barrie, Maurice Gibb, Gareth Hunt, Michelle Dotrice, Edward Woodward, Tracie Bennett, Anna Karen and so on …. It was a lovely evening. It was a sort of *This is Your Life* without the surprise. The last guest was someone I'd always wanted to meet – and I got to that night – Joan Littlewood, the legendary theatre director, famous for her work at the Theatre Royal, Stratford East. What a treat. She was so gracious and charming.

Thanks to my friend Jane Hodson at BBC GMR I landed a regular weekly gig on radio playing a Gloucestershire farmer who could foretell the future storylines of soap operas. I know! Bear with me. Jane was producer of the weekday afternoon show hosted by Lee Stone, who was great fun to work with. Lee didn't, by his own confession, watch the soaps and so I was brought in to play a comedy role – his West Country uncle Silas, one of the Cotswold Stone's (I know – shocking! And I confess that I probably came up with it because my native accent is Gloucestershire). Each Friday Uncle Silas would join Lee on the show to talk about the soaps and TV in general - it was quite popular and we did it for a couple of years.

Lee is now not only a journalist of some standing but also a novelist having written a series of books with prolific author James Patterson.

In 2020 I also got asked to go on a Podcast and on-line show called *Your Manchester* to talk about some of Julie Goodyear's jewellery which was being auctioned off for charity. The show was/is hosted by a drag queen called Belinda Scandal who is a big Corrie and Julie Goodyear fan so it made the interview really flow – and we had some laughs doing it. It must have gone well because I was asked to become a semi-regular guest on the show – and now I co-present.

That then led to me presenting my own weekly radio show on *Chatterbox Radio* for a while. That was great fun and I concentrated on songs from the shows, theatre news and often had guests, usually friends, in the studio to talk about their careers and projects. On the evening of 8 September, 2022 I was broadcasting live with theatre historian Marilyn Shalks as my guest. Just over half way through the show came the news that Queen Elizabeth II had died. I had to announce it to the listeners. Having collected my thoughts for a moment and lined up some sombre music I must admit that I shed a tear before I could make the announcement.

'Belinda' started out as a conventional singer and during a season with Cannon and Ball in Blackpool he was asked to don drag to cover for another act who'd been taken ill. At the end of the week he discovered that he was being paid more to wear the wig and frock. He never looked back and Belinda was born.

I admire him greatly. Firstly, he has worked hard to establish himself on the gay scene and secondly, he works solo. The scariest and loneliest way to work, as I know from giving my talks. I have seen him do his act many times in a variety of settings – big concert halls to small pubs. He is always professional (well, mostly) and he sings live. Brilliantly. He has also become a dear friend and along with Jane Hodson we have hosted and performed at quite a few events. Both Belinda and Jane are people I trust implicitly on stage or on air and as such there's a chemistry that can't be cheated. I think it may have been the great David Frost who said something like 'If you can fake sincerity, you've got it made.' Maybe - but if you have genuine trust and sincerity you can do anything.

'Belinda' has had me involved in all kinds of things. We've interviewed everyone from Daniel O'Donnell to Samantha Fox. There was the *Your Manchester* baking competition which we both took part in against co-presenter Michael Adams. Someone might have poured washing up liquid in someone else's batter but I couldn't possibly say more. Michael is another person I have a great working relationship with. I've known him for years – from when he came, along with a group of *Coronation Street* super fans, to hear me talk about the show. He, like novelist Glenda Young who was also there, have remained friends ever since and I am now thrilled to see him working as a national journalist.

We've done flower arranging, dancing, singing and so much more. We've even appeared in a big top with Denise Welch, Davina De Campo, Sue Devaney and Annie Wallace on a sweltering hot night. Annie plays the headmistress in *Hollyoaks* and my final appearance was with her – me dressed as a headmaster in black robes, a mortarboard and carrying cane. At the end of the show I walked back to my car in costume. A man, in his 20s, walked up to me in the car park and asked if I was working. I explained that I was. He asked how much I charged. I was just about to refer him to my agent when he explained that he'd pay by the stroke of the cane. As they used to say in the *News of the World*: 'I made my excuses and left.'

On another occasion we staged a three-hour live show at Manchester Pride (we followed a dog show – it's a great leveller being second on the bill to a poodle!) with Annie, lovely Sue Devaney, the firecracker that is Dolly-Rose Campbell and Harriet Thorpe, a delightful and radiant performer. Gok Wan even joined us! Anyway, it was my job to do all the backstage interviews and front the special show. I loved every minute of it.

When Roy died, I tried to throw myself into work. It muffled the grief somewhat. I also decided that I would do anything I was offered – Ken Dodd used to say: 'Try everything once, you never know, you might like it and then you can do it again!' He was right. I've done so many things that I'd never have done when Roy was with me. Belinda and Michael may not know it, but they've been part of that journey. I love watching them working, I love learning – and we all make each other laugh. That's what life should be about. Laugh and you won't go far wrong.

FIVE – NITA, JILL & BETTY

Roy's professional career began with a summer season residency at the Atherfield Bay holiday camp on the Isle of Wight. At the end of it he had to return to his hated day job as a draughtsman at an engineering works in his home town of Preston but having had a taste of showbiz he knew that he just had to get back into it somehow and so he started to write off for acting positions in repertory companies. Before long he got an interview, and then the job, at the New Theatre, the former Empress Ballroom, which was owned and run by Nita Valerie. Nita was a wonderfully eccentric character. In 1960 she had been cast as Ena Sharples in *Coronation Street* but was replaced by Violet Carson before the show made it on to TV screens because she had difficulty learning the lines and to cover her slips would go into improvised clog dancing.

Roy began working backstage in 1964 but was quickly promoted to actor. This was weekly repertory theatre where a company of actors would stage a different play each week performing at night and rehearsing next week's production during the day. As part of an actor's contract, you had to provide your own costumes and sometimes your own props. It was a tough life but a marvellous training ground particularly for someone like Roy who hadn't been to drama school.

Roy lived in digs, or lodgings, in the town. His landlady Amy would help with his costumes by searching high and low on the market for suitable jackets and ties each week. Her husband, Walter, was Polish and spoke very little English, so Roy was good company for Amy and her little Pekingese dog.

Nita allowed Roy a week off for his first Christmas there so that he could make a trip back home to his family in Preston, but he'd only been there a couple of days when she rang him begging him to return to the theatre. There was a crisis. One of many. Comedienne Hylda Baker had been contracted to star in the pantomime *Babes in the Wood* which was due to open on Boxing Day but during rehearsals she had fallen out with the pianist who had in turn walked out taking the rest of the small 'orchestra' with him. Nita knew that Roy could play – would he return to tinkle the ivories for Hylda?

The pantomime starred Hylda as Nurse, Nita herself as Awful Annie, Jimmy Slater as Dame, Mervyn Rolando as Hylda's mute stooge Cynthia (of which there were many over the years including lovely Matthew Kelly) and Mara Laine (impresario Paul Raymond's sister) as Principal Boy. Roy arrived back at the theatre and met the musicians Nita had managed to hurriedly assemble. Joining Roy in the pit was a drummer and a variety act billed as 'Frieda Hall and Bimbi' – Frieda was not only a popular organist of her day, she was also Mayoress of Keighley. Incidentally, she appeared in the film *Little Voice* accompanying Jane Horrocks. Bimbi was a poodle who sat on the top of the organ and howled along with the tunes. The Halle orchestra they were not.

At the first rehearsal with Hylda the trouble started immediately. She was singing *Show Me the Way to Go Home* with a 'babe' on each knee and kept insisting that the band were playing too fast then too slow then too fast and so on. At lunchtime Roy went out and bought a metronome, a wooden device with a sort of pendulum which is set to the number of beats per minute required and which pings as it rocks back and

85

forth, which he placed on the front of the stage. When rehearsals commenced this thing started going back and forth and pinging. Hylda went silent and walked gingerly towards it. 'What's that thing doing there?' 'My metronome? it marks the beat then we know we're not going too fast or too slow no matter what you think,' Roy calmly replied. 'Well, I don't want that pingalinging away like that, go pingle it somewhere else.' The metronome was packed away having done its job and she never complained again.

Nita was suffering money problems and couldn't afford to pay Hylda one week so she offered her the pick of furniture from her home and this continued for the rest of the run. Hylda used to come on stage and look down at Roy in the pit and chat to him when other actors were speaking. 'She's given me the tallboy today,' she'd mutter.

Nita was quite a personality in the town having run two theatres there, so she'd often be asked to open things or present prizes here and there. On one occasion the company were performing a three-act comedy set in Blackpool with Nita performing the pivotal role of the seaside landlady in pinny, headscarf and curlers. During the interval between acts two and three Roy passed her in the dressing room corridor, now out of her costume and dressed in an evening frock and coat. 'What are you doing?' he asked. 'Ah, I'm presenting the prizes to Miss Textiles so I'm bobbing out,' she replied. 'But you're in this next act! You've got most of the dialogue!' She explained very calmly that she'd be back before the play finished and the cast should just improvise for half an hour until she returned. And with that she was gone.

Members of the audience who had to leave early when a play went on longer than usual would walk down to the stage and shout up to Nita that they'd have to miss the ending because the last trolleybus to Fixby, or wherever, was about to go. Nita would stop the scene to acknowledge them and wish them well.

One week they were performing *Jane Eyre* in which it's vital that the audience don't know about the mad woman in the attic until later in the plot. Nita was playing this part and so was dressed in billowing rags, had her face smudged with soot and she wore a bedraggled wig. She would pace the wings listening for the audience's reaction to key passages of dialogue and weighing up how it was going. On this particular night a long scene between Jane Eyre and Mr Rochester was dragging on. Nita turned to Roy, playing the vicar, off stage and said, 'I'll have to go on and give it a lift!' He tried to restrain her telling her that she'd ruin the whole plot but she wasn't to be dissuaded – she ran on stage screeching and pinned Mr Rochester to the floor and getting a round of applause from the audience. The actors playing Jane and Rochester were stunned as Nita left the stage for the wings once more. 'Yes, that's perked it up' she declared!

On another occasion they were performing *Dracula* with members of a local amateur dramatics' society playing the many villagers. Again, Nita patrolled the wings judging how the denizens of Huddersfield were taking to Mary Shelley's' gothic classic. During one of the big crowd scenes she again announced herself unsatisfied with the pace of proceedings and grabbed a shawl and rushed on shoving some of the extras aside. Arriving centre stage, she stopped and briefly wondered what to say. She hadn't thought that far. 'Here, have you heard about this count fella going round sucking people off?' she screamed and then promptly left the stage. Once more, in disarray.

They don't make them like that anymore.

Now, I mentioned Mara Laine as one of the cast of that production of *Babes in the Wood* starring Hylda Baker. Mara was a variety act in her own right but in the 1960s she teamed up with one Jill Summers (perhaps best remembered as Corrie's blue-rinsed Phyllis Pearce) and together they toured as 'The Two Dizzy Dames', a musical comedy act. Roy remembered, when playing in the pit for the Hylda Baker pantomime, that a variety star, a singer, swathed in floor-length fur coat, visited the theatre and they were briefly introduced. That was the first time he met Jill Summers. Back in 1964.

They would meet again at Yorkshire Television when they starred in a new soap opera called *Castle Haven*. Roy was asked to audition for the role of Harry Everitt and had to travel from Manchester to London on the train. At Manchester Piccadilly he bumped into Kathy Staff who knew him from attending Oldham Rep. They got chatting and it turned out that she was auditioning as Lorna Everitt, Harry's wife. When they arrived at the audition venue there were, of course, lots of other actors waiting to read for the same roles but they were being called in in pairs. Roy and Kathy decided to go in together because they were the same height – and they got the parts.

Castle Haven was a twice-weekly late afternoon soap set in a large house which had been converted into flats in a Yorkshire coastal town based on Whitby. The Everitts, along with their two children Sylvia and Dickie, were the young family with financial problems. The cast included Sally James (later to present *Tiswas*), Gretchen Franklin (later Ethel in *EastEnders*), Jill

Summers, George Waring and John Comer, best remembered as Sid in *Last of the Summer Wine*. It ran for a year from March 1969 but wasn't shown across the whole of the UK partly because Granada thought that another northern soap would distract from *Coronation Street*, now approaching its 10th birthday. ATV only took it for a few months before replacing it with their own *Honey Lane* as the various commercial channels jostled for ratings.

Another issue which the fledgling soap faced was when, in March 1969, just a week after going on air, the Emley Moor transmitter up on the hills near Huddersfield collapsed due to strong winds and ice. A temporary mast was quickly constructed to serve some parts of the region but Yorkshire TV also had to hire a zeppelin airship to fly around other areas beaming pictures down to the ground from a special aerial. Roy and Kathy recalled that the tea in the canteen went up a penny a cup to help pay for it. I recently learnt that the top of the original Emley Moor mast is still in use – as the Huddersfield Sailing Club's race control tower.

Castle Haven wasn't the success that everyone hoped for and so after a year the series ended, and the cast went their separate ways. The show's creator Kevin Laffan was then asked by Yorkshire to create a rural soap for the lunchtime slot. At first, he refused but went on to enjoy great success with *Emmerdale Farm*. Kathy was beaten by Sheila Mercier to the role of Annie Sugden.

Jill Summers would play quite a role in our lives. Not that Jill Summers was her real name. She was born Honor Margaret Rozelle Santoi Fuller but there was no chance of that making it into light bulbs outside a theatre!

Jill/Honor was born into a theatrical family. Her mother, Mary Power, was the daughter of William and Ann Power, Shakespearian actors of Irish origin. Her mother would use different names throughout her own distinguished stage career but the one which stuck was Marie Santoi, actress, singer and producer. Marie married Jim Moss, a piccolo player, in 1896 but during their marriage she had an affair with Tom Ball (known as 'Major' in his stage act). She fell pregnant with a son and when husband Jim found out he left for the United States. That son, Tom Fisher Moss, would also become a star of the music halls under the stage names 'Signor Meneghini', 'Signor Bassani' and plain 'Tom F. Moss'. Jill's mother Marie then married Alf Fuller, a trapeze artist, who used the stage name Alf Rozelle – and he was Jill's father.

There were many, many other performers in the family including Marie's sister, Jill's aunt, Millie Grey, a comedienne and dancer, and her brother Will Power. Marie and Jim had a daughter who worked on the stage, Queenie Pickford, who in one contemporary article is referred to as the niece of legendary star Will Fyffe – and Jill's uncle was Leslie (Johnny) Fuller who was the most celebrated feline performer of his age playing the cat in all the major *Dick Whittington* pantomimes. Little Honor's destiny, along with her sisters Jose and Marie Jnr, was already mapped out for them, wasn't it?

Just a quick hop back to Tom 'Major' Ball though. Tom is of note for two reasons – firstly, he is thought by some to have been the inspiration behind the line 'Goodnight Major Tom' in David Bowie's hit *Space Oddity*. The hypothesis is that Bowie might have seen posters, perhaps in the windows of Tom's garden gnome manufacturing business (which is what he went into after leaving the theatre) for Major Tom's circus act in his native Brixton. What's a definite is that you will have heard of Major Tom's son with his wife Gwen Coates, former Prime Minister John Major.

Little Honor was almost born on the stage of the Palace Theatre, Manchester where her heavily pregnant mother was performing that early December night in 1910. However, Marie made it home to Eccles just in time. Many of the family were involved in Marie's touring shows which tended to take the form of musical scenes with exotic titles such as *A Night in Japan, Pearl of the Orient, Egypt* and *The Runaway Jap*. Sometimes Marie would put together a variety bill around these scenes, sometimes she performed within someone else's show. Here's just one of many reviews published across the UK, this one being from the *Ipswich Evening Star* of 1907: 'Top of the bill (at the Ipswich Hippodrome) is filled by Marie Santoi and her merry Japs, who pay a welcome return visit in their catchy musical sketch entitled 'A Japanese Tea Garden by Night'. The scenery and dresses are charming, and the chorus of ten girls dance and sing in pleasing style, whilst Marie Santoi was the Japanese Princess, and the indispensable Naval Officer from the ship in port make violent love to each other, despite the threats of the irate emperor who, however 'is brought to see things in a different light,' and all ends well. The excellent orchestra, under the baton of Mr Davies, acquits itself with great credit.'

Of course, despite this sounding a life of glitter and stars, it was hard work schlepping around the country never really knowing whether the next date would work out, whether they would be paid or whether the costs of travel and digs would cancel out the income. Jill often talked of having to travel ahead to the next town to parade through the streets on a cart advertising the coming attraction and we know that Marie often had to sell off, or pawn, her clothes and jewellery to keep things ticking over. Not that Jill was with her mother all the time - she and her sister Jose would be placed in 'foster care' if you like with friends and family for much of the year.

In later life Jill would always love a bargain, or even better, a freebie, no doubt learnt from these early days. In fact, she had it down to a fine art. She usually stayed, during filming, at Manchester's grand Midland Hotel and she would often invite us to meet her there for 'drinks and something to eat'. She would perch herself on a sofa halfway between the lovely French Restaurant and the toilets. When we arrived, we were told that we were having halves of lager. I didn't like lager, but she would insist as it was the cheapest drink which came with a free bowl of nuts. She had it all sussed out.

As people came back and forth, they would usually recognise Jill, partly because she had the blue-rinsed hair in real life and stop to chat. More often than not someone would be celebrating an anniversary or birthday and Jill would pour effusive congratulations on them. This usually happened as the lady, for it was usually a lady, passed us on her way to the toilets. Having given her celebrity encounter some thought she would pass us again on her way back to the restaurant. Jill would smile; conversation would start again and before you knew where you were you'd be invited to dine with the happy couple. This happened several times when I was with her and on one occasion at the end of the meal the couple in question, who loved having the starry company and her tales, proposed that we should have brandies. The host named two brandies and asked me to choose the one I wanted. I knew nothing about brandy so picked the only one I'd heard of. 'You're learning,' Jill whispered squeezing my hand. 'That's the most expensive. My mother would have been proud of you.' Praise indeed.

So Jill's upbringing was tough but it was about to get tougher. By the 1920s variety shows were on the wane and cinemas were all the rage so Marie started making her own films, silent dramas, and toured the country showing them with her and other family members, such as Tom F. Moss, singing along live. In 1924, in Bradford, tragedy struck as an account from *The Stage* of 3rd July, 1924 reports: 'The death took place on Friday of Marie Santoi who formerly toured the variety theatres with a musical and dancing scena (sic) entitled *A Night in Japan*. During recent years Miss Santoi has been working in picture houses, and she was due to appear in Bradford on Monday last in connection with the film *John Peel* but was too ill. Her condition became so serious that she was removed to the Bradford Royal Infirmary and was operated upon, but she died as stated.'

Jill was just 13 when Marie died and the life which had been the norm up until then collapsed. Her father gave up show business whilst her sister Jose entered it as a singer and dancer and then quickly met and married a wealthy man who took her to live in Egypt leaving Jill with her father. She ran the house and also had to find a non-theatrical job so worked in service and in a bobbin factory. Then Alf re-married - to a woman Jill didn't see eye-to-eye with - so she started to consider a life away from the family.

At the age of 16 she married a man double her age, Jack Hunt, and they moved to Sale in south

Manchester to run a newsagent's business on Northenden Road. Although Jill detested getting up early to deal with the papers, she loved the interaction with the customers and the shop became her stage. She also demonstrated her good head for business and converted a back room into a hairdressing salon later moving to bigger premises and launching her own brand of products under the name 'Margaret Rozelle'. Although she had no inclination to return to the stage, she knew many of the touring acts who would visit the area and she often had them lodge with her and Jack. She loved talking about her mother and the people she worked with ... the smell of the greasepaint never left her.

When the Second World War began Jill was advised that her business was a luxury one and would have to close. She would have to find herself a more suitable occupation, so she contacted ENSA and offered to return to her roots. They asked her what her stage name was and she looked at her 'gill' of beer that she happened to be drinking on the warm summer's evening and plumped for Jill Summers. So, Jill Summers took to the stage as part of a touring 'fit-up' company who toured works canteens, factories, garrison theatres, air-raid shelters and community halls – some of the companies were superb and featured big names but some were a hotchpotch of poorly paid and poorly rehearsed acts who earned the nickname: 'ENSA – Every Night Something Awful'.

By Jill's own admission she was sacked on several occasions, not for the quality of her act (she sang *I Don't Want to set the World on Fire* well enough) but because she clashed with some jobsworth or other. She had a lifelong hatred of authority which she said had been inherited from her mother.

However, a new act was soon born when she teamed up with half-brother Tom F. Moss, now known as 'The Caruso of the Hall's' thanks to his large frame, monocle, van Dyke beard and booming baritone voice. Together 'Tom F. Moss and Jill Summers' found themselves on variety bills at theatres up and down the country. Jill described their act thus: 'Tom came on singing such songs as *On with the Motley* … he soon had them spellbound. When he finished the orchestra used to strike up another number and there was an argument with Tom that it was not the music rehearsed. Then I would come on in an immaculate evening gown and open the gob. Tom left the stage, and I went into a parody of *The Pipes of Pan*. Then he returned and we did duets together, *White Dove, I'm Falling in Love* and others. As brother and sister, we knew each other so well that we harmonised perfectly.'

They were snapped up by the powerful Moss Empire circuit and booked into all their theatres. They had made it, and they were now playing the biggest theatres in the country. All except one, the London Palladium. The week before they were due there they were at the Empire, Sheffield and Tom went on stage a little worse for wear. The punishment was the cancellation of their Palladium appearance. Tom had quite an eye for the ladies and would choose one of the chorus girls at the start of the week with the sole intention of 'bedding her' by the Saturday. Jill also recounted that young mothers would often turn up at the stage door claiming Tom, usually correctly, to be the father of their baby.

How the pair split up the act, and why they split, is slightly open to conjecture as Jill, in my hearing, gave several slightly different accounts, but they all involved Tom failing to turn up at that week's venue, Oldham Theatre Royal. Jill was forced to perform solo for the first time, but she had the week from hell culminating in her being diagnosed with appendicitis and Tom, not waiting for her to recover, replaced her in the act. She also discovered that he had been taking more than his 50% share of their fees.

Jill had to have an operation and went home to Sale to recuperate, and it was during that time that she made the decision to stay a solo act. She returned to the boards at Christmas, 1947 playing one of the Ugly Sisters for Leslie and Lew Grade in Shrewsbury. Meanwhile Tom was also solo in pantomime as his new partner had left him, so Jill was eventually persuaded, at the start of 1948, to reunite with her errant brother.

Variety was dying and instead of working a different theatre each week it was now a week here, a week there and two weeks at home. This suited Jill and she enjoyed returning to husband Jack. But on 20th November, 1948 she found him collapsed on the floor in agony and he later died of a heart attack at Altrincham General Hospital. She had to work, she wanted to work, and so, within days of the funeral, she headed to Dewsbury Empire to play Widow Twankey alongside Tom, as the Emperor of China, in the pantomime *Aladdin*. Again, Tom enjoyed a drink too many between shows and Jill was asked to return the following year - but on her own. Tom was furious when she accepted.

Soon afterwards she re-married. Dr Clifford Simpson Smith was the lucky man, and the couple bought a flat in Wolverhampton. Cliff loved show business and would go on to write many of Jill's jokes and sketches. Feeling more secure now that she had someone who believed in her talents alongside her, she plucked up the courage to finally break away from the double act once and for all – Tom was becoming more and more unreliable through drink anyway. Their last joint appearance was at the Capitol, Didsbury (later the home of ABC Television).

Cliff put pen to paper and Jill developed some of her elements from the double act and slowly they fashioned a new solo spot featuring the old *Pipes of Pan* burlesque, a Blackpool tart routine quick change and a Lili Marlene spot which kept her busy, along with pantomime each year, through to the beginning of the 1950s. Eventually she was booked into a theatre she had played before but, in those days, as top of the bill. This time she was at the bottom and in the worst dressing room in the place. After a day or so the junior manager came to see her and apologised that he hadn't realised her pedigree. They became friends and he would go on to book her into many of his tours – he was Paul Raymond.

Let's quickly talk about Paul, real name Geoffrey Quinn. He came from a Liverpudlian Roman Catholic family and during the war he was sent to Glossop, Derbyshire where he was educated by Irish Christian Brothers. His first job was as an office boy at Salford Docks then he was conscripted to work down the mines as a Bevan Boy. He ran away after a day but was found by the police and completed his national service with the RAF. A self-confessed spiv he broke into show business with a cod mind-reading act. In 1958 he opened his first strip club and launched his property and adult entertainment empire.

During this time Jill landed her first TV appearance on a show fronted by Benny Hill called *Show Case* on which she performed her ever-popular 'Lady

Porteress' routine then it was back into a Paul Raymond revue tour alongside Phyllis Dixey, the famous stripper. Further tours, summer seasons and semi-regular TV appearances performing her regular sketches continued. Then, in 1957, came the big break – Jill's own TV show entitled *Summer's Here* for producer and impresario Jack Hylton with guest stars including Michael Bentine, Wilfred Hyde White, Nicholas Parsons and Claude Hulbert broadcast live from the Hackney Empire. Unfortunately, the show was put together more quickly than normal due to technical issues and the writers were changed mid series. It wasn't a success.

In 1963 Jill and Cliff moved to Ossett in West Yorkshire, which is where she was living when I first met her. She soon began playing the various working men's clubs between theatre and TV engagements. A long tour with Don Ross's *Thanks for the Memory* show soon followed. This was a tribute to the days of the music hall and starred many of the greats of that era – Billy Matchett, The Two Rexanos, Marie Lloyd jnr, Nat Gonella, Clarkson Rose, Cavan O'Connor, Randolph Sutton, Hetty King, Sandy Powell and Margery Manners. Then she teamed up with Mara Laine, whom she met at the Huddersfield Theatre where she was performing with Roy. They launched the 'Dizzy Dames' cabaret act but the clubs were changing and the act soon broke up. Jill wasn't sure what to do next … and then *Castle Haven* began and she was signed up for a year.

Next came a guest spot on the Diana Dors sit-com *Queenie's Castle* followed by, in 1972, her first foray onto the famous cobbles playing a cleaner, Bessie Proctor, alongside Hilda Ogden. And it was 1982 when she finally appeared as the feisty Phyllis Pearce.

We used to visit her, almost weekly, at her home in Ossett and then at her flat in Worsley. You just had to love Jill and I used to listen to her tales of variety acts and watch in awe as she would act them out. Here are just a few: Jill would talk in florid detail about an act called 'Miss Ellen and Mushie, the forest-bred lion' (I'm not sure I quite believed her, but Roy Hudd once assured me that the act was definitely real) which, by the time Jill worked with them, had aged a little. In fact, the lion, according to Jill, was quite elderly and somewhat toothless. I have found advertisements from the 1940s and 1950s promising 'Mushie, the only forest-bred wrestling lion with his trainer Miss Ellen – no cage, whips or tricks.'

Jill would talk about Miss Ellen circling the 'ferocious but ancient' lion until it would yawn and then she would quickly stick her head in to its toothless mouth and make out that it had attacked her. She would also let it eat steak off her chest but by now the meat was more minced beef than steak as the poor animal couldn't chew. Jill would act all this out playing the part of Miss Ellen, bentwood chair in hand, snarling at the lion 'Get back!' as she encouraged it to move. In fact, I found a review from *The Thanet Advertiser* of 1949 which reads 'Mushie the lion, who recently ate a steak from its trainer's forehead at the Palace Theatre every night for a week, performed the same act in a suburban London theatre last week, when the meat caught in the trainer's hair the lion calmly endeavoured to untangle the meat.'

Jill would also tell the tale of working with three real bears in the pantomime *Goldilocks* in which she, as the title-role, had to feed the bears from real bottles of milk. 'Oh,' she'd say with a wink. 'They used to get that excited they'd pee themselves and

99

fuse the footlights along the front of the stage.' Then there was the time she was invited to open some early motorway services on the M62. There was a shop and a petrol station and the man who owned it lived on site. Jill was invited along and there was a chap dressed as the Esso tiger and another riding a penny-farthing wearing frock coat and top hat. Jill used to act it all out of course; there was her, then the tiger jumping about and waving and then the man on the bike doffing his hat as he circled the pumps. Round and round they went waiting for someone to pull in for petrol. No one did. Then, eventually, the owner decided to go and have some lunch in his house at the back leaving Jill in charge. Round go the tiger and the bloke on the bike and Jill sits in the shop. Suddenly a coach full of football fans arrived and they came into the shop en masse and stripped the place of everything without paying and off they went. Of course, the owner then came back to find the tiger and the bloke still going round and round the pumps and Jill sat there in the empty shop. She was mortified.

Jill's relationship with Bill Waddington, who played Percy Sugden, the subject of her character's romantic desires, was perhaps a little cooler off screen than on despite having similar backgrounds in variety. This was probably not helped by the fact that Bill always claimed to have, years earlier, asked both Jill and Betty Driver to marry him without either agreeing. She was closer to Tom Mennard who played Sam Tindall in the show. He came between Percy and Phyllis setting his cap at her, which was rejected. Tom, who carried his own dog Dougal around in a shopping bag on and off screen, was also a very experienced variety and radio performer with a wicked sense of humour – he even lived for some time in a house he named 'Uppham Hall'. Jill often talked about him and his antics. She used to stay at the posh Midland Hotel whereas Tom stayed at a cheaper hotel up the road. One night, calculating that she would be in her dressing gown by this time, he summoned a taxi to his hotel. He'd had a dentist friend make a set of false teeth that were green and chipped which he placed into a clear plastic bag. He asked the taxi driver to deliver them to the Midland and make the concierge aware that they were Miss Summers' and that she had left them in an old man's bedroom at the Commercial Hotel. This happened and they were carried ceremoniously by a porter to her room – she of course, opened the bedroom door without her teeth in, giving credence to the tale. She was the talk of the Midland for some time after that.

Another time he got his taxi to call for her at the Midland on his way to the studios. The taxi driver recognised her and started to chat about the show. Then suddenly Tom threw a bunch of keys on the taxi floor with a clatter. 'Ooh I am sorry, how embarrassing!' said Tom. 'What's happened?' asked the concerned driver. 'Miss Summers' coil has just popped out!' he replied. 'You won't tell the newspapers, will you?'

Then there was the time when the newspapers were full of the fact that Andrew Lloyd Webber's *Phantom of the Opera* was coming to Manchester. Tom turned up at the Midland wearing a black bin liner and a white half mask telling the receptionists that he and Jill were off to audition for the lead roles. As she appeared the staff lined up to wish them luck.

Jill was no stranger to practical joke playing herself. In fact, her favourite was to wait until some unsuspecting guest actor was in the *Coronation Street* Green Room, where the actors rested and learnt lines, and then go to the toilet. When she came back, she'd have her skirt tucked into her knickers at the back and she'd wait to see if the poor newbie plucked up the courage to tell her or not. She also used to position herself in the Green Room so that she had a view of anyone coming in or out. She loved to get all the gossip. When she left the show due to ill health and Roy was still in it, we'd barely got through the front door of her flat before she'd shout out 'Go on then...' waiting for all the news.

Leaving the show was a big blow for her. When she died, I was honoured to be asked by Roy to write the eulogy he read at the funeral. Here it is:

'There can't be many people here today who haven't, over the past week, reflected on the time they've spent with Jill. And in particular, of the stories she told and the pranks she pulled, just to make us laugh. But for Jill, the gift of laughter was the oxygen of life itself.

'No matter where she was, the Green Room, at home or in recent months, in hospital – that space became her stage and those who passed through it became in turn, her audience or her stooges. Even, at the height of her illness, I have never heard so much laughter on an intensive care ward – nor seen so many visitors and nurses crowded round one bed. I think the record was 15, including a Staff Nurse, all hysterical, beneath a sign proclaiming, 'three visitors per bed'.

'Of course, Jill loved this and began developing routines to keep us all amused, one being her now infamous Frankie Vaughan impersonation. As you entered her room, she'd start singing Give me the Moonlight waving cardboard bowl over her head. A

prop, she very carefully kept to hand in her bedside locker should the conversation ever flag. Jill's natural ability to make people laugh earned her the love and respect of the many friends she made amongst the hospital staff and I'm sure, they gave her the courage to fight as hard as she did. That and the hundreds of letters and cards she received from fans around the world.

'Her performance as Phyllis Pearce of course, has become a Street classic. But it's for her performances off screen, in the Green Room, that she'll be remembered most by the cast of Coronation Street. Her recollections of her days in variety and the odd acts she shared the bill with would bring peals of laughter. She also loved to be party to all the days' happenings and so would sit in the middle of the Green Room, watching both doors so that no one could pass through unnoticed – and only an exchange of information ensured safe passage.

'Jill's interest in those around her was quite genuine and so, in our reflections, we must count ourselves privileged to have been counted amongst her friends and we are all richer for having known and loved her. However, her passing has undoubtedly left a void that can never be filled. Jill was unique – her warmth, affection, generosity and humour was an ever-present light in some of our darker moments. Jill was the laughter in our lives.'

I hope I did her proud. I was honoured when producer Mike Craig asked if he could re-produce it in his book on comedy greats. As I said before, Roy re-joined the *Coronation Street* cast just as Jill left. The senior cast members always had their own dressing rooms and Roy was to be allocated his original one back but he asked if he could move into Jill's and 'keep it warm until she returned. When she died, we were asked to clear it of Jill's possessions. There were boxes and boxes of things she'd 'picked up' at the Midland such as shoe shine kits, shower caps, cheese in plastic packets ... she never changed. Roy kept Jill's name on the door until he left the show in 1998.

Jill's last words were well, very Jill. A nurse asked her whether she would like something to drink: 'A cup of tea, some milk, or a glass of water?' Jill replied: 'It gets better all the time!'

Jill's was the first of the cast funerals that I went to. It was a military operation overseen by the show's locations manager, Anne Wilkie-Millar. We met at a hotel in Worsley and from there were transported by coach to the crematorium and then back again. Outside there were banks of press photographers. That was something I never got used to and Roy rarely attended actor's funerals because he hated having to walk past the lines of lenses.

There was also something about travelling on a coach full of the residents of Britain's most famous street. I always used to think back to those storylines when the Rovers' regulars would embark on a coach trip somewhere and disaster would strike. I remember sitting next to Jennie McAlpine going to Betty Driver's funeral with the coach packed full of the current cast and the icons of the past. The car in front of us cut across the tram line at St Peter's Square and ran through a red light causing a cacophony of horns – and meant that the coach pulled up sharply. What an accident that could have been! I had visions of the show having to be taken off air. But what a way to go.

I first met Betty in the mid-80s when I was at drama college in Yorkshire and then didn't see her again for just over a decade. Betty had an amazing, although in

104

many ways unlucky, career and personal life. She was born in Leicester but moved, with her parents and sister Freda, to Manchester when her father, a policeman, was transferred to the city. Her mother Nell was a pushy theatrical mum and wanted Betty to make it as a star. Freda, incidentally, was in the same class at school as Patricia Manfield who would later change her name to ... well, she had many stage names ... but eventually to Pat Phoenix.

At the age of eight Betty started singing professionally, by 10 she was working for the BBC and by 14 she was signed up by agent Bert Aza and put in a show called *Mr Tower of London* taking over from Rochdale's Gracie Fields. The show, a revue, had toured for many years starring Gracie and her husband Archie Pitts but when their marriage broke down Betty and comedian Norman Evans took over. In the audience during the Manchester run were George Formby and his wife Beryl. Formby asked Betty to appear in his upcoming film, his first of many, *Boots! Boots!,* but as Betty once told me: 'Beryl came to see me film the scene and she said to her husband 'Either she goes, or I go!'' The result was that Betty's film debut was cut.

'It took my mother a long time to get me back to work because it had shattered my confidence,' Betty said. 'But I did get my own back on Beryl some years later. I joined the Henry Hall Orchestra in 1941 and George and Beryl were guests on one of our radio programmes. Henry had the number one dressing room and I had number two and Henry asked me if Beryl could change in my room. I said that it would not be a problem. Beryl came in but looked very sheepish. Eventually she told me that she'd been a cow to me and I had to agree, telling her that she had almost ruined my career. I'm glad I got the opportunity to tell her to her face!'

Just prior to the war Betty signed a three-contract film deal but only made two films before the outbreak of hostilities caused the contract to be torn up. Instead, she joined ENSA and toured with Henry Hall. She visited Australia, Cyprus and Malta, became a recording artiste and had her own radio show *A Date with Betty*. She met and married South African performer Wally Petersen but the marriage was deeply unhappy and Wally left her with huge debts when they parted.

In 1964 she auditioned for the role of Hilda Ogden in *Coronation Street* but Jean Alexander pipped her to the part. Instead, she was asked to star in *Pardon the Expression*, a spin-off created around Arthur Lowe's character Leonard Swindley. She told me that she found Arthur a 'difficult character' to work with and unfortunately, she was injured when the script called for her to perform a stunt with Lowe. This led to her decision to retire from show business and she, and loyal sister Freda, and their father, took the license of The Cock Inn in Whaley Bridge.

'It was during that time that Harry Kershaw, the Street's producer, dropped into the pub and told me that he wanted me to join the show. I said I'd think about it, but I had to have an operation on my throat as I had constant laryngitis. I went to see the specialist and asked how long it would be before I could take on some work and he said six weeks if I didn't speak until then. In a pub that was practically impossible. Anyway, I had the operation and I went back to the pub and everyone was trying to get me to talk but Freda threatened to put a tape across my mouth. The result was that I had a much softer voice than before.

'I came into the studio that first Monday and I was so scared that my voice wasn't sounding normal - but in the show we had a wonderful man, Arthur Leslie, who played Jack Walker, and he told me not to worry. He promised that every time I had a line, he would touch my back to give me confidence. He got me through quite a few weeks doing that. He was wonderful,' she said.

That short stint turned into years and Betty Turpin/Williams stayed behind the bar of the Rovers for over four decades. Betty and Freda lived together for many years and Betty, who drove herself to the studios each day, always rang Freda to report on the journey. Now, we always think of hotpot when remembering Betty but she was in fact a vegetarian and she once told reporters 'I couldn't cook a hot pot to save my life!'

At Betty's funeral Bill Kenwright, who played her son Gordon on the show, introduced a recording of her singing. It was the first time I'd heard her do so and it was beautiful. I now have a few Betty Driver CD's in my collection. I can see why she was asked to replace Gracie Fields, the voices are notably similar at times.

Bill Waddington (Percy Sugden), as mentioned earlier, was another variety star turned actor who I got to know a bit. I worked with him a couple of times interviewing him in front of an audience of fans. Bill's mum Epsie had been orphaned as a child and adopted by a couple who owned a wholesale meats business and Epsie had been trained in the trade. However, when Bill came into the world, she and husband William were running a pub as well as a chain of butcher's shops and as a result Bill and his sister were brought up by their wider family as their parents were run off their feet.

Bill took part in several school concerts and joined the parish church choir but he had his eye on taking over the family business. He started out as a delivery boy working his way up to Assistant Manager of a shop in Oldham. One day it was announced that the shops were having a competition to dress the windows with a promotion for New Zealand lamb. Bill told me: 'I went to a second-hand shop and bought a large picture frame which I painted gold. I hung it in the window with a backing of ferns and greenery and I placed a leg of lamb in the centre on a silver tray. We only had one light bulb so that went in to light it up with the slogan 'A perfect picture from your favourite company'.' They won.

When he was 18 his father bought him a car and this allowed him to make regular trips to Blackpool where he would see the shows – and George Formby became his hero. He taught himself the ukulele and started to imitate Formby in his parent's pub. During the war he began entertaining his fellow troops telling jokes and singing popular songs. After the war he found work doing his act in the variety theatres and eventually on radio where he was billed as Witty Willie.

He met his second wife Lilian Day when they performed together in pantomime. He often used to say that he had eyes for just two ladies – Lilian and Betty Driver whom he had proposed to at one stage. As I said before, Jill Summers insisted that he'd also proposed to her and many others besides – the old romantic! TV work came along including four roles in *Coronation Street*, a play with Margaret Lockwood and Victoria Wood's *Talent*. On stage he enjoyed a long partnership with Sid James of the Carry-On films appearing in plays and on variety bills. In fact, Sid died, in 1976, on stage during a performance of *The Mating Season* at the Sunderland Empire in which Bill was also appearing. Incidentally, some years later Les Dawson was appearing there when he saw Sid's ghost in the dressing room and refused to appear there ever again.

When Lilian died Bill decided to retire but changed his mind after being approached about playing Percy Sugden. He appeared as the cantankerous caretaker between 1983 and 1997. After just three months in the role the producer, Bill Podmore, called him up to his office. Bill thought he was going to be sacked but 'Podders', as he was known, congratulated him on being voted the third most hated man in the country in a national newspaper poll. It was just what Podmore wanted.

He remarried in 1982 but the union was short-lived. His fourth marriage, to Sheila Torr, sister of the Chuckle Brothers and Patton Brothers comedy double-acts, took place in 1995. The couple lived high up on the Moors with over a couple of thousand pigs, turkeys and race horses. He died in 2000. One of my memories of Bill was when the old studios were open to the public as a theme park and in the mornings, queues would form outside the gates on Water Street waiting for opening time. Bill would often be found there selling flat caps from the boot of his car. He never lost the love of a sale.

I'm going to dart back again to someone mentioned briefly earlier, Gretchen Franklin. You might remember Gretch from *East Enders* in which she played Ethel Skinner (with her little pug dog Willy!). I met her quite a few times as she and Roy were close.

They used to go on holiday together – enjoying some wild adventures such as driving a camper van across Holland. They broke down, ended up in ditches and even chased Lionel Blair out of a club in Amsterdam. You wouldn't think it. Gretchen came from a very theatrical family. Her father had a song and dance act, her grandfather was a comedian and her cousin was *Dad's Army* actor Clive Dunn (Corporal Jones). She made her own stage debut as a teenager in pantomime then joining forces with three other girls as 'The Four Brilliant Blondes'. She subsequently went on to dance with the famous Tiller Girls.

Gradually she made the switch from dancer to featured star and then into acting. Amongst her London stage credits were Mrs Roper in Agatha Christie's *Verdict, Grease,* and *Spring and Port Wine*. Although she played Alf Garnett's wife in the pilot episode of *In Sickness and In Health* she gifted the role to her friend Dandy Nichols when the *Spring and Port Wine* producers refused to release her to film the first series. She and her mate Dandy appeared together in the Beatles' film *Help!*

A lovely tale which Gretchen told me, and which I repeat often, involves her being booked to appear in a courtroom drama being made in Manchester. She arrived at Piccadilly Station and hailed a taxi to take her to the courts. When she got there everyone was having breakfast, so she joined in and then a bell went off and people vanished off down corridors and into offices. Gretchen didn't know where to go so she stopped some chap in uniform for help and he asked her whether she was appearing for the defence or the prosecution. 'Oh no,' she confided. 'I'm the poisoner.' All hell broke loose. She'd had assumed the drama was being filmed on location when it wasn't!

Gretchen was one of the original *East Enders* cast but resigned when she was told that Ethel was being relocated to a care home. She did agree to make occasional return appearances but was always upset about how the character had been, in her view, side-lined. There was also a minor controversy when she discovered that little Willy was being chauffeured to the studios when she, as she put it, was taking the bus. Actually, Leslie Grantham often drove her to work.

I remember Gretchen's own companion, Ernie, a little hairless dog. She was devoted to him and indeed, she gave a lot of money to animal charities. She said: 'At my age one isn't buying new fur coats and diamonds. If you get that lot of repeat fees four times a year you can afford to be a bit more generous to other people.'

She died in 2005 just days after her 94th birthday. What a character she was.

Ken Parry

Jill Summers

Bill Waddington

Roy Barraclough in one of his
first dame performances

Jill Summers and her real bear

Roy Barraclough in an amateur
production in Preston

Tony Warren with a
Jayne Tunnicliffe original

Switching on Oldham's Christmas lights
with William Roache & John Jardine

Launching Kevin Kennedy's book

With Chris & Caroline Gascoyne

Interviewing Sue Devaney at Pride

Introducing Mikey North

Hylda Baker

Jill Summers in a similar costume

Jean Fergusson

Fun at the Oldham Coliseum in 1895

The cast of YTV's Castle Haven

Mark and the Mayor

About to go on stage
with Jane Hodson &
Belinda Scandal

With Vicky Entwistle

The Gilroys switch on the
Blackpool Illuminations

Celebrating with Bill & Ali Tarmey

With Johnny Briggs

Betty Driver in her dressing room

Dancing with Angelina Ballerina

Working with the Cairngorm Reindeers

Blackpool Summer Season

With Gerald Dickens

With David Neilson

Julie Hemondhalgh & William Roache

Roy, Cunard's Eric Flounders
& Thelma Barlow

Charles Foster, Meg Johnson, Mark,
Peter Riley, Paula Tilbrook & Alan Rothwell

Filming with Belinda Scandal &
Simon & Emma Gregson

Reporting for Your Manchester

SIX – JILL & HYLDA

It was Jill Summers who got me interested in variety theatre. She always had a little stack of *The Call Boy* magazines at her side (I do now). *The Call Boy* is the magazine for members of the British Music Hall Society who have been 'championing the cause of the history of popular entertainment since 1963.' 'We are here,' they say 'to make sure that nobody forgets where we came from!' – something I heartily agree with and I'm proud to be a member – just like Jill was.

I've already written about Jill and her amazing life and how she entertained me with tales of life on the boards. Here are just one or two more - there was the moment she sought revenge on a star who had been a little bit too 'handsy' so she shoved a potato up his car's exhaust pipe and left him in a gloomy car park in sheeting rain trying to work out why his motor wouldn't start. And the event she went to with Lynne Perrie (Corrie's 'Poison' Ivy Tilsley) who had insisted on buying a new frock from Harrods. It was stunning – decorated with thousands of beads and pearls. Lynne was getting ready in her hotel room when she found to her horror that the frock was too long but as a car was coming to pick them up in less than an hour there wasn't much that could be done so Jill got hold of a pair of scissors and cut a foot off the bottom of the frock.

When they arrived at the venue they were immediately whisked onto the dance floor and as Lynne was spun round by her suitor hundreds of beads were cast across the parquet flooring and fellow dancers skidded and slid in every direction. Lynne was furious!

Lynne was quite the character. Having worked the clubs all her life she found the fame of being on the cobbles - and the wages - almost startling. If she saw something new in a shop window she just had to have it – and others played on this. Johnny Briggs, who was a very close friend of hers, might see something in a shop that he wanted so he'd encourage Lynne into buying one for herself. He knew that she'd get it and then not know why she'd bothered and get bored. She'd then offer whatever it was to her friends and he'd likely take it off her hands.

She'd often, between scenes, remember that she needed something – say, a loaf – for home so she'd phone for a taxi to go and fetch a loaf and bring it to the studios. But she'd then go and film a scene and forget about the loaf so at the end of the day she'd come out and find a taxi had been sat there with the meter running for hours. The loaf would cost her a hundred smackers!

Jill would also entertain with stories of unusual and slightly outrageous acts. Now, I have checked all these out and they absolutely did exist even though to today's ears they sound fantastical. 'Professor Sparks and Thelmina' were one such act (their real names were George and Thelma Rathbone apparently). The act was based on electricity – at one point George would light up his wife by placing light bulbs in her mouth and running an electric current through her. 'He blew all her teeth out one night,' Jill told me. 'She just got false ones and carried on!' What a trouper. The finale involved a metal bath full of water and a doll, again made of metal, dressed in baby's clothes. Audience members were challenged to bath the baby. As soon as they got their hands in the water an electric current was run through it and they'd be thrown backwards dropping the doll. You couldn't do that now – nor would you want to I imagine. The act retired in the 1950s and George and Thelma opened a TV shop near Warrington.

Joseph Pujol was presented under his stage name 'Le Petomane' and he was a French flatulist (or professional farter!). By taking in large amounts of air often using a pump – but let's not dwell too much on that - he could manipulate his body so that he passed wind on cue. The act involved him imitating cannon fire and thunderstorms, but he became known for farting to music with *O Solo Mio* and the French national anthem being favourite pieces. He concluded the act by blowing candles out from several yards away. Many people recall the television play about his life which starred Leonard Rossiter and was written by Galton and Simpson.

I met June Elliott, a former acrobat, and the widow of singer GH Elliott, in the 1990s when she was living at Brinsworth House, the home for retired members of the entertainment industry (the Royal Variety Show is held to raise funds to make it possible) and she talked to me about life in variety - touring the world. We tend to look back on variety with rose-tinted glasses but for the performers, particularly by modern standards, it was a hard, very hard, life.

Wilson, Keppel and Betty often evoke fond memories from modern audiences. The two men, Lancastrian Jack Wilson and Irishman Joe Keppel, met when both worked for Colleano's Circus in Australia. In the 1920's they travelled to Canada and America and they met up with Betty Knox who joined them. The act was born. Capitalising on the craze for all things Egyptian (the tomb of Tutankhamun was discovered in 1922) they developed a dance routine known as *Cleopatra's Nightmare*. The two men were costumed in sandals, very short nightshirts belted at the waist (as they got older these, thankfully, got longer) and often wore fezzes. They would scatter sand on the stage and perform their mock Egyptian dance with the rather beautiful Betty. It's perhaps worth noting that there were many Betty's over the years. The original one leaving to become a celebrated wartime journalist who covered the Nuremburg Trials. Incidentally, when they appeared in the Middle East I'm told they took their own sand!

They were regarded as one of the finest speciality acts of their generation appearing at several Royal Variety Shows, Palladium seasons (alongside Frank Sinatra in 1950) and world tours until the act retired in 1952. Not everyone liked them, however. When they appeared in Berlin in 1936 Joseph Goebbels, then Minister for Public Enlightenment and Propaganda, described them as 'indecent' but then he isn't exactly remembered for his insight into showbusiness, is he?

Another lovely tale before we move on. Jill was switching on the Christmas lights on in some Northern town. There was a stage constructed outside the Town Hall and a microphone connected up to speakers on lamp posts in all the neighbouring streets. The lady mayor made a short speech and then turned with her back to the microphone to say a few words to Jill. Jill said: 'There was this little girl next to me, I think she'd won some competition to be there, anyway the mayor bent down to speak to her and right at that moment farted - right into the microphone. This noise, like a trumpet voluntary, echoed through all the speakers in all the side streets. She wasn't embarrassed at all – she turned back to the microphone and just said, 'Oh, hark at me!' and then introduced us! It was the best introduction I've ever had!'

One person Jill rarely talked about was Bolton-born comedienne Hylda Baker. Jill explained that when she started out, she often wore a check suit and a tatty feather boa. Appearing in a two-theatre town on one occasion she went along to see what the competition were up to and she was astounded to see Hylda performing her 'Cynthia' act (tiny Hylda did the patter stood next to a tall, lanky and mute stooge). Hylda was clad in a check suit and feather boa. Jill immediately went back to her digs and telephoned Jimmy James who was known for his 'elephant in the box' routine with Eli Woods and Roy Castle. 'I've just seen that woman,' she said. 'She's doing our acts – wearing my costume with your dumb sidekick stood there.' Jill would never forgive her.

In a 1948 tour called *Bearskins and Blushes* Hylda had indeed taken her first female stooge, Mary Radclyffe, who played her prim and proper friend. It was her then husband Tex Martin, a film stunt man, who played the first mute Cynthia. 'I had broken every bone in my body doing it,' he said of his stunt career in an interview. 'I suggested I help in her act playing Cynthia. There was no money in the business then and we fell on hard times, we had a little old car and we kept trying. Finally, we started on the up and up. I stopped my stunt work and concentrated on my part as Cynthia. I did it for ten years.'

The 'feud' lasted until Hylda's death in 1986. Until then Jill studiously avoided appearing on the same bills or at the same charity functions as Hylda. I also recently learned that 'Two Ton' Tessie O'Shea once complained that Hylda was performing part of her act – Hylda cut the routine.

Hylda Baker was a complex character. Her father, Harold Baker (known as Chukky Baker), was a part-time comedian and dancer whose day job was as a painter and sign writer – and sometime, scenic artist. Hylda, later known as 'The Little Napoleon' and 'Little Miss Sure Shot,' was the first of seven children and partly earned her billing because she grew to just 4ft 10 ½ inches.

At the age of 10, in 1915, she made her debut at the Opera House, Tunbridge Wells (now a Wetherspoons) and from then on continued to tour as a solo act. In 1924 tragedy struck the family when her father was touring in a show which involved a 'get the ghost' routine. This involved sand bags being dropped from above the stage just missing the performers. For some reason this particular week the management put iron weights in the bags. During the fateful performance a bag fell wrongly and hit Harold on the head splitting his skull open. Blood was pouring everywhere.

Some idiot decided to pour liquid plaster into the wound to stem the flow of blood. Harold became seriously ill with blood poisoning and never worked again. For the rest of his life, he would suffer severe headaches and sudden personality changes. There was no compensation, no insurance. He was admitted to a hospital (in those days called an asylum) where he stayed for the rest of his days.

Having slogged around the country with her stage act for 40 years Hylda was 'discovered' when she starred in an episode of the BBC series *The Good Old Days*. This led to her own series *Be Soon*. She would go on to appear on television and on cinema screens in some classics including *Oliver!, Saturday Night and Sunday Morning* and *Up The Junction*.

In 1968 she began a five-year run in Granada TV's *Nearest and Dearest* with Jimmy Jewel. The pair, as brother and sister Eli and Nellie, didn't get along and, as mentioned previously, the other artistes suffered in an atmosphere of mistrust and competition with, as the series went on, Hylda having to read more and more of her lines from boards and Madge Hindle having to give her cues during the filming.

There was no doubt that Hylda could be … prickly. Her father was still in the asylum, and she kept that a secret terrified that if the public found out then her career would be ruined. She also travelled around with her pet monkeys, Co Co and Mickey, who quite frequently destroyed theatre dressing rooms.

She loved the public adoration and there's a classic story of her appearing on stage in *A Taste of Honey*. As she made her first entrance the audience applauded so she went down to the front of the stage and acknowledged them: 'Thanks, I didn't know if you'd recognise me in this get-up!'

In 1972 she was surprised by the show *This Is Your Life* (produced by Oldhamer Roy Bottomley who, along with Tom Brennand contributed to *Nearest and Dearest* and wrote the spin-off *Not On Your Nellie*) during rehearsals for *Nearest and Dearest*. Her agent Bill Roberton, actor Jack Douglas' brother, who was in on it, collected her from the rehearsal rooms in the Thames TV limousine supposedly to take her to a press event. It all went a little bit wrong.

The journey was quicker than expected and by the time they reached the studios in Euston Road they were running too early so the driver did a quick turn into Camden Town. Unfortunately, they now found themselves stuck in nose-to-nose traffic and were likely to arrive late. Having thus far driven at a decidedly stately speed the driver put his foot down and they hurtled around back streets trying to catch-up the lost time. Hylda grabbed Bill, frantic, and shouted that they were being kidnapped. She was genuinely terrified. Only when they pulled up at the studios and she caught sight of Eamonn Andrews did she start to calm down.

Watching the episode now you can sense Hylda's fear. No doubt Hylda had a few skeletons in her cupboard however the researchers had been kind. The only issues were the appearance of singer Dorothy Squires with whom there had been some disagreements and Tom Hardy, at that time the actor playing Cynthia. Hylda wasn't pleased that he appeared on the show as she always felt that the Cynthia's should remain in the background.

Hylda went on to star in a spin-off *Not On Your Nellie* with Sue Nicholls, Wendy Richard and John Barrett (subsequently replaced by Jack Douglas) however it was short-lived and beset by issues. As I've said, she found it difficult to learn the lines and began refusing to attend rehearsals. During the filming of the third series she slipped on some beer on set and broke an ankle. She was written out of the next episode and the final ones were cancelled. She also sued LWT which didn't help the relationship.

In 1978 she and Arthur Mullard released a version of *You're the One That I Want*. Again, there were issues. She caught sight of a poster on which he received top billing and she caused a scene. Billing had been a reoccurring bone of contention and there are lots of stories of her climbing ladders outside theatres with a tape measure to make sure the size of letters used to spell out her name matched the contract. Maybe some of this is apocryphal but there's no doubt that working with her was 'awkward' at times. She had fibbed about her age for much of her adult life, so she was older than people realised and she was developing Alzheimer's.

In 1981 she moved to the artiste's retirement home, Brinsworth, and then in 1984 to a psychiatric hospital. It was here that she died aged 81 two years later. A sad end for an amazing force of nature and hugely talented woman and to say otherwise but be simply – to use one of her catchphrases - *ricidudilous!*

SEVEN – THE REP

I've already shared a few stories about the
Coliseum, but it played such a big part in our lives that
it deserves its own chapter. If you've not been to
Oldham, then you need to understand that it's a few
miles from the centre of Manchester and is a former
mill town. Well, a mega mill town really – in fact it had
so many mills that there was one, at least one, for
every day of the year. It was even nicknamed 'Spindle-
opolis'. When Roy first went there, he was amazed to
find that it was raining black rain. The atmosphere
was just so polluted by all these hundreds of chimneys
belching thick black, rancid smoke into the air.
Kenneth Alan Taylor told me that on his first day there
he was travelling by bus to his digs. He could see snow
on the bus windows and yet it wasn't snowing. What
he was seeing, floating about the bus, and on people's
coats and in their hair, was the cotton residue from
the mills.

Of course, eventually all that came to an end but
during their time at the Coliseum (or 'Rep' as it was
known) Theatre in the 1960s and '70s the town was
still making and exporting lots of product. The theatre
itself was first built elsewhere in the town – and as a
circus. The wooden structure was then moved, lock,
stock and plank, down the hill to the delightfully
named Fairbottom Street where, over time, it was
converted into a cinema and then into a theatre.
Because it was designed as a circus the circle curved
round in such a way that the view looked down onto
the stalls rather than at the stage, a historic echo of
the times when the stalls were a circus ring and the
circle went right round the interior of the auditorium.

Can I just digress? Again? Kenneth Alan Taylor once told me about the Queen Mother visiting Oldham in 1977 to open the Queen Elizabeth Hall. Ken was acting as Master of Ceremonies, and he swears that the Queen Mother was given the key to open the doors for the first time. She turned the key in the lock and pulled on the door handle to open the door, but the doorknob came off in her hand. Without batting an eyelid, she turned to the mayor proffering the knob with a smile. 'I believe this is yours,' she said. Now back to the plot ...

Flicking through the programmes in the theatre's archives gives you a veritable who's who of acting talent who all trod the boards across the decades. Amongst them Eric Sykes, Bernard Cribbins, Frank Middlemass, Jean Alexander, Meg Johnson, Ray Moore, Anne Kirkbride, Pat Phoenix, Ralph Fiennes, Minnie Driver ... the list goes on. Repertory theatre gave actors the chance to play lots of different roles, some they weren't suited for at all, under great pressure. To learn their craft. Learning scripts quickly turned out to be great training for working in soap operas. Roy always used to say that it wasn't the learning of a script that he found difficult it was forgetting the one you'd done the week before.

By the time I went to work there things were different. There was no permanent company of actors although we did have some regulars and there were guest directors. In my time they included Malcolm Hebden and Alan Rothwell as I've mentioned earlier.

We produced about eight of our own shows each year under Kenneth's management with visiting shows in between. These I was largely responsible for booking. A programme made up of one-nighters and week-long runs of touring plays. They included Ken

Dodd who always sold out within minutes. Doddy was notorious for the length off his ... now, now missus ... his shows but if you went round to see him in the dressing room afterwards, as I always did, he'd do another hour whilst Anne, now Lady Dodd, packed everything into the car. I booked Hinge and Bracket, for whom Roy played the regular role of Teddy Tranter in their radio shows, which turned out to be their final live gig. George and Patrick, the talents behind the ladies, gave a fabulous show and we went out for dinner afterwards – but Patrick, Dame Hilda, obviously wasn't well. Sadly, he passed away only weeks later.

The place had a fabulous history and occasionally I would be asked to appear on TV or radio talking about it. I've already told you about the ghost and the *Mystery Hunter's* show but just before I left, we had a call from the makers of *Most Haunted* who wanted to film an episode in the theatre. The star of the show in those days was the psychic Derek Acorah. I was a bit sceptical – a researcher came and explained that they'd like me to take them through the history of the building, tell them who I thought might haunt the place and then promise to cover up all the old pictures so that Derek wouldn't get any clues on the night. They made me the promise that they wouldn't tell him anything in advance. I wasn't actually there for the filming, but I was interested to see the show.

Derek communicated with quite a few of the people I had mentioned in my briefing and got some of the salient facts wrong as well – such as the fact that Harold Norman didn't die on stage, he died in hospital some days after the accident during the production of *Macbeth*. I came across a few psychics over the years – I booked one chap in for an evening show at the theatre. His posters arrived with the strap line 'His accuracy is amazing!' under his name. Unfortunately, his name was spelt incorrectly.

I was introduced to Sally Morgan who is now very famous name by a friend who was working with her at the time. As a result, Roy and I went to see her at the theatre in Stockport and at a private dinner party. Whatever you think of psychics – and I keep a healthy scepticism although I am open to any possibility – I have to admit to being truly amazed by something she said to me. We were on our own, and she never referred to it again, but she told me that my grandfather liked the comedy magician Tommy Cooper. The significance, which Sally couldn't possibly have known anything about, was that my paternal grandfather suffered a stroke and was never able to speak again. The last time I saw him, was the day after Tommy Cooper had died on stage in front of millions of TV viewers. Gramps wanted to tell me that he'd seen this and so mimed Tommy's distinctive 'Just like that' hand gestures.

When I wrote my book *They Started Here!* (some wag quipped that quite a few careers ended there too and they weren't wrong!) I was fortunate to have the support of lots of friends who contributed anecdotes so let me share a few with you:

'During the war when male actors were scarce, I was playing the title role in *Jane Eyre*. Playing opposite me was a Rochester who was much too old and doddery for my sixteen-year-old Jane. I remember that when Rochester proposed to me an old lady in the audience shouted out: 'Don't Dora love – he's far too old for you!'' Dora Bryan

'They mounted the production of *Marlene* and my favourite moment every night was watching the front of house people coming in to watch me sing *Where*

Have All the Flowers Gone. My brightest memory is of the fire alarm going off after the show one night – I, confused and in my dressing gown, stood in the doorway of my dressing room saying, Where's the exit? No answer. Bedlam. Then the wardrobe team went rushing past saying 'Where's the dress? Save the dress!' It warms my heart to remember. Priorities!' Dame Sian Phillips

'As everyone knows Oldham winters can be very bad and I remember that in 1969, I had digs with the wonderful Mrs Bibby (£5 a week inclusive of a meal after the show, breakfast if you made it yourself and Sunday lunch with all the trimmings!). I woke up one morning to find two feet snowdrifts and I had to dig my way out of the front door. There was no bus service, so I walked, or rather fell, into Oldham panicking all the way that I'd be sacked for being late. On arrival at the theatre, by which time it was getting on for lunchtime, I found it locked and deserted – I was the only one who'd got there!' Jean Fergusson

During the days of weekly rep, it was quite a pressured environment – no wonder then that Saturday matinees were usually seen as fair game for playing pranks and letting off some steam and the audiences knew what to expect. Roy had something of a reputation in this regard and there are many, many stories I could tell but let's just have a few of the best. He shared a dressing room with the actor John Jardine, a most wonderful man and great friend, but who was less relaxed before a show than Roy so the perfect 'victim' for his pranks. In the tense thriller *Wait Until Dark* Roy's sinister gangster Roat is terrorising a blind woman as he and his henchmen search her flat. One of the henchmen was John. The search scene began with John opening a series of drawers one by one. In each one he found a gherkin. This was not normal. Roy urged him on – search the cabinet. More gherkins. The bedside cupboards. More gherkins. John was struggling to keep a straight face. Roy had no trouble; he had of course placed all the gherkins around the set. Eventually John got to the end of the search scene without giggling. Just. Then Roy held up a finger and beckoned his henchman towards him. On the finger – a hollowed out gherkin. That was it, John 'corpsed'.

On another occasion Roy had directed John in *There's a Girl in my Soup* warning John that there was to be no high-jinx on the Saturday especially as he wouldn't be there to supervise – he was going to a rival theatre's matinee in Manchester. In the play there's a long telephone scene where John had, in effect, to speak to himself. At the matinee the telephone rang as usual, John picked it up and started his dialogue. Then suddenly there was a crackle at the other end. Then Roy's voice: 'Oh, there you are you old ham...' Roy was in the sound box at the back of the theatre watching the stage, but John had no idea where he was. John continued with the script, holding the phone away from his ear. 'Don't try that Jardine. I can see you!' and so it continued. Afterwards John asked to see Roy in his dressing room – back came the reply: 'The director doesn't see artistes between shows. That wouldn't be professional.'

John and Roy were friends from 1966 right up until Roy's death in 2017. After that John started to call me every evening at 7pm, just a few words, and that all important question 'How has your day been?' – it means so much to me. We still do it. That's one of the hardest things to lose when you say goodbye to a partner. A quick glance, someone to ask you how you are, someone to tell something to, someone to share a joke with, to reminisce with, to say to you 'Is that all?' when you're worrying about something, to burst your pomposity or to bring you down to earth, or to say, 'Well done!' John thoughtfully filled some of that void. And I will always be grateful that he cared so much to do that for me, and Roy.

In 2023 lots of us gathered at the Coliseum to bid it farewell. I can't really tell you why the funding was pulled – because I can't be sure which story I've been told is entirely true. Christopher Eccleston called the theatre 'a cathedral for working class entertainment' – indeed. But in my view buildings are about the people in them and the Coliseum has witnessed some amazing people on stage and behind it, has launched thousands of careers and brought pleasure to millions. It was heart-breaking to sit in the auditorium and watch the curtain fall for the last time. Since then the seats have been stripped out, the fittings moved on to new homes. I hope that it will come back in some form or another ... you know, not all change is good.

EIGHT – OH YES IT IS!

Being taken to the annual pantomime at the Bristol Hippodrome certainly made its impact on me - and I always love it when pantomime is done properly and with care. That first visit for a child can mean so much - and can be life-long. For me the theatre was cobalt blue skies, red velvet, glittering gold, the sound of a live orchestra, the conductor on his rostrum almost jumping up in the air on the beat as he conducted. It was another world.

Were you lucky enough to be taken? Do you even know what pantomime is? It has its origins back in medieval Italian theatre when troupes of actors toured the country performing well-known morality tales. Because each region had its own dialect, they performed in mime so that they could go anywhere people were willing to pay to see them. Actors specialised in roles – the old man, the squire and so on, much as happens in pantomime today. They'd set up on the village green (even today actors backstage will say 'See you on the green' meaning on the stage), and they would have dug out a bit of a ditch to sleep in (actors call their lodgings 'digs') and after the show someone would go around with a box to collect any donations (that's why you book theatre tickets at the box office).

This type of theatre was called 'Commedia dell'arte' and featured characters such as Harlequin who indicted his mood by pointing to the colours on his costume (green for envy and so on) and slapped a stick across his palm at key moments (slap stick!). These characters eventually arrived in London where they were anglicised and pantomime (which means 'imitator of all') took off. Over time rhyming couplets

136

were added and then proper dialogue and eventually, thanks to a take-over by the stars of music hall, the Harlequinade element slowly vanished and pantomime became what it is today. Pantomime has always adapted to the times and to audience's tastes.

In days gone by if a performer got a panto contract and a summer season contract they had the year laid out. I remember dear Ken Parry saying that every actor should receive a call from their agent telling them that a theatre wanted them to star in their pantomime. Then they should get a call to sort out how large they'd like the letters outside the theatre spelling their name out to be. Then they should get a call asking how much they wanted to be paid and how they'd like their dressing room to be. Then they should be shot. They've had the best of it. I know what he meant. Pantomime is a tough gig on stage and off.

The big stars tend to be signed up in the late spring then auditions and casting follows until the whole creative team is put together. The big star might have a chat with the script writer about any particular routines or songs they want to go in and eventually the cast meet to start rehearsal in November. There'll have been a photo-call for the local press – Cinderella arriving in her coach, actors trying to climb a beanstalk, that sort of thing. These are always a little fraught – the costumes are never ready, the actors haven't met before, it's a wet day in July ... I remember overseeing one for a production of *Aladdin*. One actor went to the wrong town, the costumes came but we had no wigs, hats or shoes and the rickshaw lost a wheel. I cobbled together a gold casket full of beads and bangles and a tiny plastic lamp purchased from the Disney store. As three of the cast stood, semi-costumed, outside the theatre in a cold breeze, a dustbin lorry reversed into the photo. It was hardly magical. Another time the photographer wanted someone dressed as a cat to sit on a wall. The actors refused as the wall was too high for comfort. Guess who had to don the ears and whiskers?

After rehearsals, which often take place in a church hall somewhere, is the arrival at the theatre, usually on the Monday of the week you're opening the show. Dressing rooms are allocated on a 'the bigger the star the better the dressing room' basis rather than 'the more costume changes the nearer the stage you are' basis. If you're sensible you travel with your own kettle, mug, milk etc and you turn your dressing room into a little flat as you'll not be seeing much of your home/hotel/digs for the next few weeks.

Tuesday is usually technical rehearsal. That's a really long (sometimes more than a day) rehearsal which concentrates on the lighting, sound, scenery changes and so on. It can go long into the night and the actors are really required to make their entrances and exits over and over again whilst technical staff try and ensure everything runs smoothly.

Thursday is the rehearsal for the cast, hoping that the technical issues are all sorted. It's also when timing is tested – is the show too long? Can the scenery changes be made in time? Often, cuts are made – and for some people that means you have less and less to do. In some cases, it means adding an extra bit of nonsense (known as a 'Joey Joey' after the great 18th century clown performer Joey Grimaldi) to pad things out.

Friday is opening night.

That's how it should go. Roy had a couple of panto adventures when things didn't quite go to plan. The

1985 panto at Stockport's Davenport Theatre was *Aladdin* starring John Inman in the title role with Roy as his mother, Widow Twankey (the name is a joke on the eighteenth-century inferior Twankey Green Tea) and Jack Douglas. Near the end of the run Roy got a call from Nottingham Theatre Royal to say that Billy Dainty, who was playing Twankey in Nottingham, had been taken seriously ill and was having to leave the show. Could he help? So, he completed his last night at Stockport and then travelled down and appeared in a second *Aladdin* with little rehearsal, a new script, new songs and a new set of costumes. And with Barbara Windsor as his son this time.

He also stepped in at the Manchester Palace in 1995. Roy had decided not to do a panto and he'd been booked on to the QE2 as a guest speaker. Mr T of *The A Team* TV show had been booked to play the Genie in Manchester's *Aladdin* but hadn't, for some reason, flown in from the States. Would Roy play Widow Twankey? This meant that the actor engaged to play the dame would have to stand down and there would have to be a complete juggling of roles. Roy agreed to do it and with just a few days' rehearsal he opened in Manchester.

Those few days were a bit of a nightmare. I was in the dressing room trying to help out; we also had two wardrobe staff who were making new costumes in there – and eventually a live duck – and regular visits from a slavering and deeply lovable Schnorbitz the Dog who was appearing in the show with magician Richard de Vere.

It was Richard's fault we ended up with the duck. Not just any duck – Desmond the Death-Defying Duck no less. Richard had devised a routine to perform with Mr T where he placed a duck inside a small cannon (I can't remember where it fitted into the plot – if at all) and fired it across the stage and through a picture and then had it vanishing. Anyway, this was achieved by the real duck going into a black bag … *sorry, by magic!* Roy was holding the picture and had to, on cue, press a switch which caused a duck-shaped hole to appear in it. The duck wasn't actually ever fired you'll be glad to know. Well, I sat in the auditorium to watch this spectacle being rehearsed and it soon became apparent that it wasn't going to work. The duck didn't like going in the bag at first and kept sticking his head out, the cannon which had a mechanism to make it waddle as if the duck was inside, fell off the table and the button on the picture frame jammed and then flicked open so that the picture flew out of Roy's hands and high into the air. Roy looked down at me with a pained expression and we both shook our heads. Desmond was axed - and he spent the rest of the panto in the shower cubicle in our dressing room. He was quite happy and went through plenty of corn.

I mentioned the 'wardrobe team'. Roy knew Charles Alty from his amateur days in Preston. Charles then came to Oldham to run the wardrobe department at the Coliseum before opening his own costumiers and fancy-dress shop in the town. He made many of Roy's pantomime costumes and stored them between seasons. He lived over the shop, and I well remember going there to discuss new costumes. There were several doors which opened into his lounge, and he would sort of clap his hands and assistants would enter with rolls of fabrics and throw them out across the room. It was like a souk. Charles was also known for sometimes being late in delivering the finished items. John Jardine was doing pantomime in Worthing one year and Roy offered to lend him some dame costumes which Charles had to despatch. John, not known for his calmness, kept ringing to find out where they were. Charles insisted they'd been sent. Then John got a call from the theatre in Eastbourne asking why they had a skip full of costumes waiting there for him. They'd been sent further along the coast.

On another occasion we were going to see Joe Longthorne in his show at Southport and Charles was coming with us. When he got in the car, he had a costume in his hand and asked if we could detour to an arts centre on the way. Then he sat in the back and produced his needle and thread explaining that an actress was opening in a show that night and he would try and finish the dress before we got there. I had sympathy for the actress waiting for her frock.

I think the worst thing that happened to me in pantomime was a production of *Aladdin* when, during the cave scene when Aladdin rubbed the lamp and there was a huge burst of flames and smoke, the backcloth was accidentally set alight. All good fun. I do like the story of Aubrey Phillips' production of *Ali Baba* in which, to save money, they had one actor playing one of the 40 thieves and the rest painted on a piece of scenery. This resulted in the glorious line 'You come with me, the rest of you stay there and don't move!' As if they could. I remember two chaps telling me that they'd done a tour of *Cinderella* for him but that the wrong scenery arrived, and they had to make do. The ballroom scene had to be set on a ship.

Anyhow, the hard work of pantomime is that you're doing that tough, long, and sometimes very boring 'tech week' and then bang! The show's open and you're performing it twice a day. Or more. Now I know people who work in mines and factories and so forth will all be screaming 'you think prancing about on stage is hard work...' but it is. The main reason is the wave – you come in, sometimes at nine in the morning, ready for a 'schools' performance' at 10.30, get into your make-up, your wig, your costume (if you're a dancer the first of maybe a dozen – or the dame, the same) and you wait. It starts. You're required to be at the top of your energy levels for an hour, then there's a 20-minute lull when you make a cup of tea and usually change into costume number nine. Then off you go again at the top of your powers and then stop. Two hours when you can't go out because you're wearing make-up and have a microphone sellotaped to your head, you manage a sandwich and another cuppa, and you wait. And then off you go again.

If you get a cold or flu. Tough. You take precautions of course but every time that curtain goes up, you're face-to-face with a thousand or more coughing children. You're singing right at them, you're a target for every germ in the place. On stage it's baking hot thanks to the lights, the wig and the costume and every 15 minutes or so you strip off in a cold corridor and put something heavier on. No wonder most of the cast will come down with something. During that intense period, you're all thrown together and usually something team building happens. As with any pressure-cooker situation, it kills you or makes you stronger. You feed off the audience's energy – and sometimes when that doesn't come – maybe the audience have come through the snow, or they don't really want to be there or there aren't many of them – then it kills it. Roy, when playing dame, would sometimes come back to the dressing room after his first entrance and shake his head. The audience weren't up for it today. He would then ceremoniously remove one earring. 'They don't deserve two,' he'd say. Incidentally, he always wore two pieces of jewellery given to him by former Corrie colleagues – a pair of diamante earrings from Pat Phoenix and a necklace which had been gifted by Lynne Carrol (Martha Longhurst).

In the 1990s John Jardine, Roy and I were chatting about the pantomimes they'd written for the Coliseum some two decades earlier. The scripts were pulled out from the back of a cupboard, and we read through them – they still worked and with a few tweaks here and there and a bit of de-Oldhaming we decided to try and have them published. I added to these three with some scripts of my own (for some years I'd been asked to adapt various panto scripts for amateur groups), and we were lucky enough to find an agent willing to handle the royalties. As a result, they were produced from Auckland to Aberdeen.

I leave you with one final panto tale – oh, yes I do! Michael Barrymore was starring in *Aladdin* at the Opera House in Manchester whilst *Les Miserables* was playing at the larger Palace Theatre up the street. One wet matinee an elderly couple emerged from the auditorium at the Palace and asked to speak to the manager. They explained that they hadn't exactly not enjoyed the show so far, but it was 45 minutes in, and Michael Barrymore still hadn't appeared – and that's who they'd come to see. They were sent down the road for Act Two.

Oh, and a bit of advice I was once given by Welsh pantomime dame extraordinaire Wyn Calvin – always put your dame bra on the radiator! Good advice. Diolch.

NINE – WEATHERFIELD & HIGHGATE

I've mentioned earlier that I've looked after quite a few groups of overseas *Coronation Street* fans over the past couple of decades – accompanying them around the studios and the various filming locations. I've hosted many dinners at which cast members have made 'surprise' appearances too. These have included Barbara Knox, Johnny Briggs, Julie Hesmondhalgh, Chris Gascoyne, Vicky Binns, Jennie McAlpine, Mikey North, Malcolm Hebden, Antony Cotton, Craig Gazey, Debbie Rush, Joe Duttine … an awful lot over the years.

The cast are always so good with the fans and take time to chat – and no doubt answer the same questions over and over again – as they move from table to table. I only had one actor – who will remain anonymous – who gave too much away. Asked who he liked working with the most he revealed who he didn't like and why. Asked whether he enjoyed working on the show he replied that he didn't and then laid aim at various departments. He left the show not long after. Luckily it was in the days before social media, so no one found out … and my lips are still sealed.

Sometimes we would take a group to see an ex-cast member in a theatre show which was always fun and for quite a few years we would take the coach out to the Broadoak pub in Ashton-under-Lyne to listen to Bill Tarmey singing with his band.

I often asked friends to call in at the group's hotel at breakfast time and so various behind-the-scenes people would drop by for a chat. One such guest was an on-screen regular. Jim Whelan started out as an Extra (they're called Supporting Artistes these days) on

Coronation Street but in 1973 he landed his first speaking role. He played the postman who delivered news of a windfall to the Duckworths, the vicar who buried Lisa Duckworth, Rev. Todd who Tony Gordon invited round to offer words of comfort to Carla on Liam's death, the vicar at Steve and Karen's wedding – and many more. He agreed to come and talk to my group at their hotel – and he went down very well indeed. I think it was that success which spurred him on to write his autobiography and start giving talks. You'll have to read his book *Imposter* – it's a fabulous account of life as a jobbing actor. And you must look out for him on the cruise ships talking about his career.

Someone else who I've got to know very well is Hayley Cartwright. Hayley played the recurring role of Corrie's celebrant. She's officiated at naming ceremonies for Oliver Battersby and Alfie Franklin, buried Lewis Archer, tried to marry Aidan and Eva and did marry Jenny and Jonny Connor. We first met on the set of *Your Manchester*, the weekly on-line arts show, and we've been friends ever since. Hayley is a real-life celebrant now so you can be married, buried or named by Weatherfield's finest. She's a lot of fun and we've worked together in a big top, on a coach, on TV and on radio.

One unusual request from a pair of Canadian fans was that I stage a Corrie wedding for them. Well, a blessing actually. They were part of a *Coronation Street* holiday group from eastern Canada. We kept it a secret from the rest of the group which involved smuggling the couple away so that when the group arrived at Ryecroft Hall, which doubles as Weatherfield Registry Office, they were waiting in the wedding outfits – and flowers by Canadian celebrity florist Neville McKay. Canon John Sykes, a friend, agreed to carry out the blessing which had a Corrie theme. It was lovely watching the happy couple leave to the strains of the famous theme tune.

I've heard the theme played in a variety of locations. The grandest being the Liverpool Philharmonic Hall by the combined talents of the Liverpool Philharmonic and the Halle Orchestra for Granada's 40th birthday. The theme was composed by Eric Spear who had previously composed the theme for *Biggles*, which Tony Warren had already written for. He died just six years after the show launched but his name continues to be used in the credits to this day which must make him one of the most credited people in television history. When the show celebrated its 50th birthday we staged a special service at St Mary's in Prestwich, which doubles as Corrie's church, with the theme being played on the organ, prayers of thanks for the cast and crew, and lots of mice! The parishioners had knitted lovely church mice (each named after a Corrie character) which were given to each of my Canadian fans to take home with them.

The first time I ever spoke to a group as myself, rather than playing a part, was at Highgate Cemetery in London. I'd been working for London Transport and one of the perks was free travel so each weekend I'd use this to visit lots of out of the way corners of the capital. One Saturday I got off the tube at Archway and strolled up Highgate Hill past the statue to Dick Whittington's cat, and through the lovely Waterlow Park. Through the trees I could see a church-like building. This is the Victorian chapel at the front of the cemetery.

There are approximately 170,000 people buried across two cemeteries – one dating from 1839 and the other from the 1860's. Amongst those lying at peace here are some fascinating names – Charles Chubb (the lock and safe maker), Charles Cruft (of the dog show), David Devant (magician), Catherine Dickens (the famous writer's wife), John Galsworthy, Radclyffe Hall, Beryl Bainbridge, Douglas Adams and George Eliot (the writers), Bob Hoskins, Patrick Wymark, Jean Simmons, Sir Ralph Richardson, Corin Redgrave, Tim Piggott-Smith (actors), George Michael and Hutch (singers), Christina Rossetti (poet), Frank Matcham (theatre architect – whose deigns include the Bristol Hippodrome where I started my love of live entertainment), Bruce Reynolds (mastermind behind the great train robbery), Max Wall (comedian), Karl Marx (philosopher) and so many, many more. Even I had a grave there at one time but I sold it when I moved up north.

The cemetery was opened by a private company, The London Cemetery Company, and it is as wonderful for those famous names buried there as it is for the curious – the menagerie owner whose tomb is topped by a lion, the boxer who has a huge statue of his bull mastiff guarding his last resting place, the horse atop the grave of Queen Victoria's official horse slaughterer, the soaring draped urn topped plinths, the obelisks and haunting, ivy thronged, angels ever reaching for the sky, the catacombs and Egyptian avenue of resting shelves. As a cemetery gets fuller and the site needs more care, so the finances no longer work and in the end the owners gave up on the place. A group of locals banded together to save it and it's now run as a charitable trust. For a year or two I got involved – serving as secretary for a while and giving guided tours. I'm still, if you'll pardon the irony, a *life member*.

Amongst my favourite stories that I told on my tours – the Druce family who got caught up in a series of court cases to determine who was actually buried in their vault and the murder of Eliza Barrow by Frederick Seddon made it into my second book *The World of Crime* and they still feature in one of my talks today. The cemetery gang was an eclectic mix of people whom, largely, I enjoyed working with very much. I spent quite a few Halloweens in there too. There were often rumours of people planning to break in on Halloween and to guard against this the police would carry out quite a large operation with dozens of officers stationed around the site. A number of us volunteers, who knew our way around in the dark, would stay to assist. By and large nothing much happened but I think the police enjoyed it and they often used it as a training exercise for the dogs – and new young officers. I lived close to the police station at the time and the coppers would give me a lift home in the van. My neighbours, leaving for work, often raised an eyebrow as I was thrown out of the back of a police van on a murky November morning.

One of my fellow guides was involved in the ancient ceremony of the Swearing on the Horns and I was invited to take part. This is a curious bit of historical nonsense really, but it does entitle me to call myself a Freeman of Highgate. It took place on Saturday 31st March, 1990. A party of us, led by my friend in powered wig and carrying a pair of ram's horns on a staff, plus the Mayor of Camden, in full robes and chain, set off to walk the boundary of the borough. At various public houses we stopped to take a drink and make an oath. It goes a little like this: 'To drink to a man when a woman is near, You never should hold to be right, sir; Nor, unless 'tis your taste, to drink small for strong, Or eat brown bread when you can get white, sir, Manniken, canniken, good meat and drink are pleasant at morn, noon and night, sir.' No, I didn't understand it either.

I recall that those of us being sworn in had to pay a fine which went to charity, and we got a certificate which lays out our privileges. If I remember correctly these include kissing wenches, drinking in alehouses on Christmas day and the power to kick a pig out of a ditch in order to sleep there unless there are three pigs and then only the middle one can be turfed out. I, thus far, haven't invoked any of these rights but you never know when it might come in handy. But none of that is why I remember the ceremony so vividly. As we neared the completion of our day-long walk, in glorious weather, around Camden, we made our way down Charing Cross Road and as we started to turn left towards Covent Garden we became aware of police helicopters, plumes of smokes and lots of noise in the distance. There were no mobile 'phones so we didn't have a clue that we were heading into the Poll Tax Riots. Suddenly the mayoral car pulled up with a screech next to us and the council attendant got out and relieved the mayor of her chains of office. He drove off with them – as all mayors will tell you the security is for the chains only. We completed the last bit back to the council offices as quickly as we could.

When my first book *They Started Here!* came out I was asked to give a few talks promoting it. Today I have a menu of a dozen talks – from Victorian crimes to the Titanic's survivors, variety acts to pantomime, *Coronation Street* to cruise ships. I've spoken to hundreds of groups down the years and raised quite a bit of money for charity doing so. Sometimes it's been for large groups – over a thousand – and some for just a handful. The smallest group I've ever spoken to was based in a church and when I first went there I was surprised that the audience comprised just three ladies. They asked me not to tell anyone about them – they didn't want any new members. They explained that a member had died leaving the club quite a lot of money. Everyone had now died off so there were just these three left and they were having a grand time spending the cash.

Sometimes I get to talk at dinners and sitting at the top table I've met some very interesting people. One was the Salford painter Harold Riley. He told me this lovely story – one of my favourites. He and LS Lowry were walking through the West End of London when they came across an art gallery. In the window were two paintings – one attributed to Lowry and the other attributed to Harold. Neither man had actually painted them, so they went into the gallery to tell the staff. 'Excuse me,' said Harold to the young assistant. 'In the window you have a painting by LS Lowry and one by Harold Riley. Well, I'm Harold Riley and this chap in your doorway is LS Lowry – and we didn't paint them.' 'Oh, I see,' said the young man. 'Thank you. We'll have to get a second opinion of course!'

It was also good to chat with Harold about his friendship with Tony Warren, *Coronation Street's* creator. Harold and LS Lowry often took walks through Salford with their sketch books and there's a brilliant sketch which pops up now and again on social media of Archie Street in the Ordsall district. It stood just behind the Tudor Ordsall Hall – the hall still stands but the street is long gone. At one end was St Clement's Church and at the other, a corner shop.

When *Coronation Street* began, Tony and designer
Denis Parkin toured Salford looking for a street that
they could use as inspiration for the look of
Coronation Street – and it was Archie Street that fitted
the bill perfectly.

In fact, the opening shots in the early credits are of
Archie Street and Harold Riley told me that he was
there when they were filmed in December, 1960
alongside Tony Warren. In 1968 the real residents of
Archie Street moved out and it stood empty until 1971
when it was demolished. St Clement's Church still
stands and that also goes down in Corrie history – in
October, 1963 it was used for location filming for the
wedding of Jerry Booth and Myra Dickinson.

On another occasion I was sat next to a senior
military man who entertained me with stories from his
very distinguished career. He was very, and justifiably,
proud of having met several members of the royal
family and we swapped a few stories. One of his was
overhearing the Queen talking about Princess Anne
and saying 'Her favourite breakfast is smoked salmon
and scrambled egg. She didn't get that extravagant
taste from me!' I told him about Roy going to the
Guild Hall in London to celebrate ITV's 50th birthday.
Laid out along a picture gallery were lots of poseur
tables, the sort of ones you find in coffee shops, with
groups of ITV stars gathered around each one. Roy
was at the last one and the Queen arrived and worked
her way down chatting to each group. When she got
to Roy's she said 'Ah, 50 years, how marvellous.' He
told her that he'd worked for ITV in every one of those
50 years. 'Oh!' she exclaimed, 'To do the same job for
half a century.' 'Well, you can't talk, can you?' He
answered her before she laughed heartily – and left.

He was awarded the MBE not long after so she can't have been too upset.

There's a similar tale that the variety comedian Tommy Trinder used to tell. He'd appeared on stage before the Duke of York in Scotland. The next day the abdication caused the Duke to become King George VI. A year later Trinder appeared at another royal gala and afterwards the King had a few words. 'Since I last saw you,' said the King, 'You've really done very well.' 'You've not done so bad yourself,' replied Tommy with a wink.

Sometimes I get asked to do book signings. For the launch of *The World of Crime*, myself and my co-writer Peter Riley, travelled the length and breadth of the country. The format was that we'd arrive in a town around lunchtime and do some radio interviews then pose for a photo for the local paper normally in a cell somewhere or a police museum. Then we'd appear in a bookshop during the evening surrounded by giant posters of ourselves and piles of books. In front of us would be rows of chairs for shoppers to sit and listen to a 20-minute talk before the signing.

Sometimes you'd have a full house if the publicity had worked, sometimes just a few. Occasionally, no one. As the staff realise that you're not going to be a draw they drift off and you're left to creep out into the night once the hour is up. In Leeds, on a very wet night, we had no one. Then, suddenly, all the chairs filled up, so we gave our talk and then invited the attentive crowd to step up and buy. As one they all left. It turned out that they were a party of Italian tourists who were waiting for their coach and had taken shelter from the rain. They hadn't understood a word we'd said. The publishers told us to sign all the books even if no one turned up. This, I later learnt, was a rouse. If the copies didn't sell then the shops were stuck with them – our signing them meant that they were 'spoiled' and couldn't be sent back. It helped the tome to rise up the bookseller's charts.

I've also written many, many articles for magazines and newspapers. This began when Peter Riley, with whom I wrote the book on crime, introduced me to the editor of *Lancashire Life*, the county magazine. It led to me writing for them, almost on a monthly basis, pieces covering the county's history and heritage.

Then Peter, his wife Donna, and I set up a monthly entitled *On The Air* which was published in Canada and covered British television. That led to us launching *Summer Wine Special* in this country and we were given exclusive access to the filming of the world's longest running sit-com *Last of the Summer Wine*. I knew many of the cast already – Kathy Staff, Jean Fergusson, Dora Bryan, Keith Clifford, Jean Alexander and so on which made it easier. Now we spent time in the pretty town of Holmfirth each spring and summer watching all kinds of madness being filmed and interviewing the cast between takes.

I do remember going to dinner at a hotel in Huddersfield that the cast stayed in during filming. At my table were Thora Hird, Dora, Jean Fergusson, Juliette Kaplan, Frank Thornton and Peter Sallis. At a nearby table sat Stephen Lewis, who preferred to eat alone. The waiters danced attendance (there were no other diners in the restaurant) whilst performing their own slightly irreverent camp cabaret. As they took the orders one would say to the other things like: 'We so enjoyed the soup on the Titanic!' Outrageous! I always remember the advice Thora gave me when we were talking about my public speaking. 'Don't do things for nothing otherwise people treat you like that's what you're worth!' she said. She was right – never undersell yourself.

I then became editor of a monthly magazine covering north east Manchester called *Fourmost*. It was a free lifestyle magazine and we had a large team of regular writers – Luke Dyson on travel, Barbara Daly-New on fashion, Derek Abrahams on interiors and so on. The truth was that they were all me and I used to write a whole raft of articles every four weeks. I once produced a large spread (as Barbara) on wedding fashion trends for the coming season. I'd done some research but it was hardly my specialist subject. However, when the advertising sales team visited a local bridal shop they greeted the article with some enthusiasm and asked whether Barbara could visit the salon and meet brides to be at their upcoming open day. She couldn't – so we had to kill her off.

I also got asked to host a lot of events. In Oldham, when I was at the Coliseum, we worked with the shop owners to theme the town's Christmas events programme to the pantomime. It worked very well – and we even had our own temporary radio stations. We had Aladdin FM, Cinders FM – and yes, Dick FM. I would co-host the switch-on of the Christmas lights with Jane Hodson and play Santa in the annual parade.

One year it was decided that I would play a pantomime dame in the town's TV commercial – I spent a day running up the High Street in heels. The result wasn't just a commercial but also billboards bearing my photo. I was asked if I would accompany the mayor to unveil the first of these on the main road into the borough from Manchester. It was arranged that I would change at the council offices and travel with the mayor in his official limousine. At the billboard they had me up a ladder with a bucket of paste and the mayor holding the base of the steps. Again, I was in heels!

Afterwards we were driven back to the mayor's parlour where he offered to fetch some tea. He went off to organise that and I'm sat there in full make-up, polka dot dress and yes, those heels. But I'd removed my heavy wig. Suddenly the double doors burst open and in walked a group of men followed by one of the councillors. He was showing them around and expected to see the mayoress. His party of dignitaries got quite a shock! As did I!

I loved doing the Christmas events – and we had real reindeers for Santa's parade which made it very popular. The parade drew very big crowds and it took a lot of organising. One year, 2001 I think, we had a big outbreak of foot and mouth and it was forbidden to move livestock across the country. The reindeers always came from the Cairngorms and because of the restrictions we couldn't have them, so we needed an alternative to pull Santa's sleigh. The chosen solution was donkeys. When the news broke there was much hilarity and I even had to go in full costume – red suit and beard – to a near-by farm to be photographed for *The Sun* with my magical red-nosed donkey.

For my last Santa parade, I invested in a new wig and beard. It was rather lovely – very luxuriant and it came from a firm in Hollywood. I dressed in the red suit and my new hair and I went to the shopping centre loading bay where the reindeers would be penned up. Before climbing into the sleigh, I would always let them smell me so that they were relaxed. As I approached, they started to get a bit jittery. In fact, more than jittery – I think they fancied me! It turned out that my beard was made from yak's hair and the reindeers could smell another animal in their vicinity. It got so rough in there that I had to dash off and spray a load of Silvikrin on it to mask the whiff of yak.

TEN – JOHN, DANNY & PAUL

Hanging in my attic are lots of pantomime costumes including one of Danny la Rue's, some of mine and some of Roy's – including his dame's padded bra which is full of birdseed. No balloons or socks, the birdseed, Roy and Les always contested, gave the correct weight and movement. So, there you are. Mind you, after a long pantomime run under hot lights, it did have a tendency to sprout and need a trim with a pair of nail scissors.

A friend of ours kept many of his panto frocks and accoutrements at home but suffered a dreadful house fire. When the assessor came from the insurance company, he and his wife had to go through a list of things destroyed or damaged in the fire. There was a long list of dresses and wigs. The assessor turned to the lady of the house and commiserated on the loss. 'Oh no,' she said. 'They're my husband's but he doesn't use them anymore – not since he's retired.' I wonder what he wrote in his report.

Roy used birdseed whereas John Inman used breastplates. Nowadays we see lots of Ru Paul hopefuls debate breastplates over padded bras – the breastplate is a formed latex chest. John was the first person I ever knew to wear one and it allowed his pantomime dame to occasionally have a plunging neckline. John was meticulous about his appearance on and off stage. We often travelled to see him in panto – Wolverhampton, Newcastle, London. We always had a lot of fun with John - and his husband Ron. They were great friends. Roy and John were both born in Preston just a fortnight apart so it's hardly surprising that they shared similar childhood memories and backgrounds.

We socialised with John and Ron fairly often and visited their home in London's Little Venice quite often. One thing I certainly remember was the size of the gin and tonic's John used to pour. It's no wonder I gave up drinking! I remember Roy visiting them one evening on his own when he was appearing at the Palace Theatre, Watford in a play. He had gone to Little Venice for dinner and was then catching the last train back to Watford. In the early hours I got a call from a clearly sozzled Roy at Beaconsfield Station wondering how to get back to Watford! He didn't have to tell me where he'd been – I knew he'd been Inman-ed!

John often entertained with tales of *Are You Being Served?* – from the suits on the Grace Brothers set having sleeves removed or the seat of the trousers slit to stop the actors taking them home to the stories about the cast.

One of my favourite stories of John's was when he was touring the Far East and as was his usual pattern, he needed to telephone his mother back in Blackpool each Sunday. He booked the call, which in those days had to be made by an operator dialling and connecting from country to country. It was a long process. Eventually the 'phone rang and his mother, Mary, answered. 'Hello, it's John…' 'John who? Where are you?' 'Dubai!' 'Good bye!' replied mother putting the phone down. John said that it was lucky he hadn't been in Oman.

He would often answer the 'phone and say 'Darling, I'm sitting here surrounded by frocks!' in those famous light Lancashire tones so familiar from his catchphrase 'I'm free!' He also enjoyed ringing me up and pretending to be other people with a variety of accents – and he was very good at it. He caught me out many times. There was the man carrying out a survey into nicotine damage to wallpapers, a producer wanting me to work on a musical about Blackpool landladies, a survey into weevils, and so the list goes on.

John's father had a barber's shop in Preston town centre but barbering wasn't for him and he always had a hankering for a career in show business so the family moved to Blackpool to run a boarding house. It was there, aged just 13, that he made his professional debut on Blackpool's South Pier in a play called *Freda*. However, upon leaving school he chose to embark on a career in retail starting at a big store in Blackpool and then, aged 17, moving to London to join Austin Reed. He also took in sewing work for stage performers to contribute a little more towards his rent. In 1969 he made his West End debut in the musical *Ann Veronica*. Adapted from a novel by HG Wells it had music and lyrics by Cyril Ornadel and David Croft. Despite a cast including Arthur Lowe, Hy Hazell and Ian Lavender it wasn't the success everyone hoped for, and it closed after just 44 performances. Other London shows included *Salad Days* and *Let's Get Laid* (which he convinced his mother was about a poultry farm).

Jeremy Lloyd, who had already been enjoying success with *Dad's Army*, and BBC producer David Croft, worked on an idea submitted by Lloyd who himself had worked at a store in London. The one-off episode, entitled *Are You Being Served?* was to be broadcast as part of a BBC *Comedy Playhouse* series of pilots. However, the powers that be decided, having seen it, not to give it an airing and it was filed away.

When, in September 1972, the Munich Olympics were disrupted by an attack by the militant group the

Black Panthers the BBC found itself having to fill air time which had been allotted to sports. In the scramble to find non-offensive programmes to fill the gaps they came across *Are You Being Served?* and that's when it first aired. A series was then commissioned which was broadcast from March, 1973 although Bill Cotton, then BBC Controller, insisted Mr Humphries be dropped. Perry and Croft refused.

John's experience in clothing stores would now come into its own as the flamboyant Mr Humphries. He once told me: 'There was a definite pecking order in the shops and the older ladies often had pink or blue hair. It was wonderful – we used to stand in the windows with labels on us reading 'a small deposit will secure' and wait absolutely still until groups of girls passed and then we'd move and make them scream! There was this hierarchy which was such fun.

'Comedy has to be based in truth,' John told me. 'The cast were all fairly established stage actors and we knew that each one had a turn at the funny lines so we all got on well. David was very clever – he invented the 'cut to reaction' shot so that if there was a funny line or visual gag you got the laugh from that and then he would turn the camera on whoever was also in the scene for a facial reaction so that you got another laugh. That was quite a new idea.'

In 1985, after 69 episodes, the show came to an end. 'We ended on a high and wherever I go people ask, 'Are you free?' and I smile and say, 'No, but I'm reasonable.'

John was a master of pantomime. Watching him do his dame's striptease routine as Nurse/Widow/Dame Wanda (the name she usually went by) really was a masterclass. He had a wicked sense of humour on and off stage. As well as pantomime he also made lots of appearances in music hall shows and on the famous BBC series *The Good Old Days* usually paying tribute to his idol Frank Randle. Randle was a variety comedian who got into great trouble for his antics partly because he was a heavy drinker. His most famous character was 'The Old Hiker'– an elderly chap in walking gear, high forehead with unruly tufts of white hair, missing teeth and a walking stick. His catchphrase was 'I'll fettle thee!'

Well, John often did a tribute to Frank looking just like the old chap. One time I was travelling on a train with him and the ticket inspector came along checking tickets and passes. John, immaculately attired, took out his ticket and his Senior Railcard. The inspector checked it, stamped the ticket and gave it back. John was furious. On the railcard he didn't have a picture of himself as himself - but dressed up as the Hiker. 'He didn't bat a bloody eye, did he?' he cursed.

It came as quite a shock when he was taken ill just as he was about to begin his run in *Dick Whittington* at Richmond in 2004. Luckily, Malcolm Lord, who usually appeared alongside John, took over the role. Sadly, John died in March 2007. His funeral was held at Golder's Green Crematorium and Roy and I travelled down to London the night before. We had arranged to meet a few people in the pub opposite Golder's Green Station with a view to walking to the crematorium together.

There were quite a few 'names' assembling in there by the time we arrived, and everyone fell into sharing tales of John. A lady of a certain age, whom we didn't know, sidled up and started chatting. She explained that she'd once worked with John and that she was wearing red knickers for him. We never found out the significance and indeed, I did wonder if she was at the wrong funeral. But then she started to tell us that she'd been very friendly with Cardew 'The Cad' Robinson and that she'd worn her red knickers for lots of famous funerals – Kenneth Horne's, Bud Flanagan's and Jimmy Jewel's amongst them. 'They were all here at Golder's Green,' she said. 'Oh, good,' replied Roy. 'We'll walk with you - you'll know the bloody way then!'

One of the last people to arrive was Juliette Kaplan, who played Pearl in *Last of the Summer Wine*. She'd got lost and then couldn't find anywhere to park her car. As she sat next to me in the pub, all of a fluster, she said 'Well, I just kept thinking, if I'm not there on time they'll have to keep him on a low light!' John would have loved the joke. Eventually this gaggle of British comedy greats set off on foot up the Finchley Road and round to the towered crematorium.

Frank Thornton, Trevor Bannister and Wendy Richard were all there from *Are You Being Served?* along with creators David Croft and Jeremy Lloyd. Within two years Wendy herself was gone. Now they all have moved on to the great department store in the sky. As we took our seats Burt Kwouk arrived looking for a space. He didn't look that well and indeed winked at us as he told us he didn't think it was worth his going home he felt so bad. We sat with Bill Cotton and in front of us were Barbara Windsor and Danny La Rue.

Danny was giving one of the eulogies and at that time he was a little unsteady on his feet. In fact, Jean Fergusson, who also spoke, was a bit concerned about him so as he stood, raising his then considerable frame off the pew, she put herself in a position to be ready to jump up in case he needed a steadying hand. As it happened, he made his way comfortably to the front

163

and took his position next to a large free-standing wooden candle stick on which stood a large lit candle. As he began to speak, he tottered a little, Jean ready to pounce, but then as he picked up some pace he grabbed at the candlestick, which wasn't attached to the floor, and they both sort of danced together. We all waited, hearts in our mouths, for the lit candle to slide off the top but no; candle, stick and Danny clung together until the end. As Dan sat back in his pew, he sensed we'd all been worried. 'Oh darlings, I'm a trained dancer!' he laughed.

Afterwards we all repaired back to John and Ron's lovely house in Little Venice where Danny held forth about – himself - mainly. There is a lovely story which legendary producer Dougie Chapman once told us. Danny was appearing in Blackpool for the summer season and had his little Chinese Hairless Crested dog, Jonti, whom he believed was the reincarnation of his manager and partner, Jack. One day Danny got in to his head that he wanted to buy Jonti a birthday present, so Dougie had to help him sort it. The gift, Danny decreed, should be a knitted dog coat but not just an off the peg one, something made to order. Dougie spent the day ferrying Dan around wool shops trying to locate the correct wool. When he found just the thing, the lady running the shop enquired as to why he wanted it. 'For a birthday present for my little dog,' replied Dan telling her all about the gift. The lady offered to knit it for him if he could tell her what size the dog was – or, even better, bring Jonti into the shop the next day. Dan turned on his heels – 'And spoil the surprise?' he exclaimed.

I remember Roy telling me that Danny was doing summer season in Blackpool one year and on the day of the launch for landladies (in those days the artistes had lunch with the B&B landladies to ingratiate themselves so that the landladies might suggest their guests go and watch the show) Roy and Les were filming a TV special about the resort. Anyway, Dan had done his launch and then joined them for dinner. Dan was very upset and flustered, the launch hadn't gone well. He'd been asked why he liked Blackpool and had replied that the place was so beautifully vulgar. The landladies had taken exception to what he thought was a compliment. Mind you, during the filming of their programme Les and Roy had asked a landlady why she thought people were going abroad and not coming to Blackpool for their holidays so much. She replied that she couldn't understand it, but people didn't seem to want to rough it these days.

On another occasion, a tribute lunch in Blackpool for John Inman, Dan and I shared a limousine to the venue, the Winter Gardens. We were driven along the promenade whilst Dan waved at the public walking past. Then the car broke down and we had to walk the final couple of streets! Dan told me: 'If people ask, we'll say it was planned. A royal walk-about darling!'

At the beginning of this book, I talked about going to the Bristol Hippodrome to see the pantomimes. The one that I can still see in my mind most clearly was *Aladdin* starring Danny back in 1980. Danny could come over as a bit of a caricature in interviews – he had that deep, theatrical, fruity voice. The hair was always done, he had the jewellery and the clothes that screamed showbiz. His world was showbiz. I was able to sit him down once and tell him how fantastically brilliant he was as a performer – and he was. He looked a million dollars, always. He could sing, he could dance, he did lightening changes and he didn't short-change his audiences. He was of an era but my goodness me, what a performer and what a lovely, caring man he was – he had the biggest of hearts … and, as he often used to say, he had a little bit tucked away.

The first time I met Paul O'Grady was when we were invited to attend the opening night of a show produced by a friend at the North Pier in Blackpool. That was back in 1996 and *The Lily Savage Show* also had Sonia on the bill – and a 23-year-old fairly unknown tenor called Russ Watson (now better known as Russell Watson). Afterwards we spent a long, long – but very enjoyable – night with Paul. Paul and Roy both loved a good moan – which always ended in laughter. They also got bored quickly and that led to a great deal of banter between the two. When they got going it was very funny to listen to!

When he came to Manchester to play Miss Hannigan in *Annie* he invited a few of the *Coronation Street* cast to see the opening night and afterwards Liz Dawn invited us all back to her pub The Old Grapes which was right next to the theatre, the Opera House. Paul was a huge fan of Corrie and was invited to visit the set, which he loved. I have a gorgeous picture of him in the Green Room – laughing - of course.

The next time was at Liz Dawn's wedding anniversary party at the Victoria and Albert Hotel when Paul compered. He was such a lovely chap – funny but sensitive. He was about to play the Wicked Queen in *Snow White* at Birmingham and he invited a few of us to go and see the show and stay for a day or two. Cliff Richard and Hank Marvin were also staying at the hotel as Cliff's tennis tournament was taking place at the same time. We had quite a few laughs over breakfast.

Then Paul suggested a visit between Christmas and New Year. This time we found that the hotel was actually closed to the public, so it was just a small group of us – and Buster, Paul's now famous dog – staying there. It was wonderful – we had takeaways delivered and had the run of the place. There was a Presidential Study which President Clinton had used when he'd stayed the hotel for the G8 summit of 1998. We took it over for fish and chip suppers.

A couple of years later and *Snow White*, also starring Sherrie Hewson and Kris Akabusi that year, played Southampton. Again, we went to see it. My memory of that visit was us all going to an Italian restaurant on the waterfront and the actors playing the dwarves dancing on the table as we ate. The most bizarre, and hilarious, events happened when Paul was around. What a loss it was when he died in 2023.

ELEVEN – LES, KATHY, CISSIE & ADA

Les Dawson first hit the TV big time with Yorkshire TV's *Sez Les,* which debuted in April 1969 as a Sunday late night cabaret style show, with Brian Murphy appearing in some of the sketches and the Syd Lawrence Orchestra providing the music. The director for that, and most subsequent series', was David Mallet who later achieved perhaps more fame as a director of pop music videos for artistes such as David Bowie, Queen, Blondie, Cher and Tina Turner. The second series was broadcast at the end of 1969 and series three in 1971. Brian Murphy had now gone and John Cleese had joined.

Roy, by now, had quite a list of TV credits to his name including *Coronation Street, Z Cars, Nearest and Dearest, The Lovers, Never Mind the Quality Feel the Width, Hadleigh and Queenie's Castle* starring Diana Dors and written by Keith Waterhouse and Willis Hall. He also had a very good agent in Michael Summerton. Michael represented Noele Gordon, Sinitta, Bonnie Langford, Hot Gossip and so on. He had been an actor and was one of the original Daleks in *Doctor Who*. He used to tell of going to the BBC to audition and being asked to move about the studio in a bin on wheels! He also, at one time, represented an actor called David Jones who fancied himself as a pop act. Michael listened to him sing and told him there was no future in it. Jones changed his name to David Bowie and didn't do half bad.

At some point Roy and Les met in Yorkshire TV's canteen. Roy's version of how he came to join Les was that he was eating in the canteen when David Mallet came to talk to him. They needed someone able to appear in the sketches with Les and they thought the pair would work well together. Either way, in late 1971, they filmed series four which was broadcast in early 1972. The press noticed a change with James Towler in *The Stage* writing 'Suddenly it's happened – Yorkshire have discovered what show business is all about.' He remarked that Les looked more relaxed and that 'Dawson is big enough of an artist to share the laughs, in this instance with actor Roy Barraclough whose bona owner of a china boutique was a gem.'

Sez Les moved from the late night slot and, if you like, became the family comedy format that most of us remember. Les and Roy became firm friends off screen as well as on – but why did they get on so well? I think it's because they had very similar backgrounds.

Les Dawson Jnr. was born in Collyhurst in Manchester in 1931 living with his parents, Les and Julia and Julia's parents. Yes, Les' dad lived with his mother-in-law – as would Les Jnr in later years! Both Les, like Roy, was an only child.

At junior school Les Jnr. wrote a poem entitled *A Winter's Day* which included the line: 'Mantles of white gentleness caress a sullen earth.' Bill Heatherington, his teacher, called him up in front of his class and praised his efforts. From that moment Les Jnr. wanted to be a writer. He could write – and he could make people laugh. 'I was small and chubby, I could pull side-splitting faces and I had a gift for mimicry,' he once said. At the time children took an exam, the 11 Plus, which determined what happened next – whether they went to grammar school or not. Les failed his but Roy wasn't even entered for it – the headmaster telling him that he was too 'chubby' to sit exams. So, both men followed the same path.

Both also left education at the age of 14 and took apprentices. Roy as a draughtsman, as we've learnt, and Les started at the Co-op in Manchester working in the drapery department as a general dogsbody hauling skips of parcels around. He was earning 21 shillings a week and found it 'soul-destroying'.

We know that Les took up the piano – his first act was a singer-accompanist. When he was conscripted in 1949, he was posted to Germany where he played in the Officer's Mess, and after he ended up in Paris where, legend has it, he found a job playing in a brothel. Roy also learnt to play and again, his first professional contract was playing in the bar of a holiday camp. Both struggled to break into showbusiness, and both ended up back at their original, more mundane, jobs. For Roy the big break, such as it was, was joining Nita Valerie's company at Huddersfield in 1964. For Les it was appearing on TV talent show *Opportunity Knocks* in 1967 although he didn't actually win his series, but he did win the audience vote and this led to a few offers of other TV work such as an appearance on a show called *The Blackpool Show*. Dickie Henderson hosted and The Shadows were the top of the bill with Les right at the bottom, but it was that night, I would argue, that Les broke through.

I have a rare recording of his act that night and there are some familiar lines and topics including: 'I've been in this game so long that I remember when *The Archers* just had an allotment', there's a gag about mice and mouse traps and references to poverty. But no mother-in-law gags – they came later.

1969 would be a turning point for both Les and Roy as they both began working at Yorkshire Television's new Kirkstall Road Studios in Leeds. The station went on air for the first time in July 1968, so things were still exciting and new. Roy was signed to star in the soap

Castle Haven and Les was signed for the first series of *Sez Les*. Interestingly, both series aired their first episodes in April 1969, but it would be two years before they were contracted to work with each other.

Les' first producer was John Duncan, who was already producing the channel's *Roy Hudd Show* which was written by David Nobbs (who then also wrote for Les), Keith Waterhouse and Willis Hall (most known for *Billy Liar*), Peter Tinniswood, Michael Billington and John Antrobus. David Mallet was appointed director, as mentioned earlier, which proved a masterstroke. David's experience with video editing (a very new skill he'd learnt in the USA) allowed him to let Les record more material than was needed – usually 50 minutes' worth at a time, which could be edited down to 25. This suited Les and gave him an advantage.

Les was also signed up for the pilot, and subsequent series, of *Joker's Wild*, a hugely popular comedy panel game show hosted by Barry Cryer with regular team captains Ted Ray and Arthur Askey with Les often appearing alongside Arthur and Al Martine alongside Ted. Incidentally the show was created by stand-up comics Mike King and Ray Cameron, whose son is comedian Michael McIntyre. It's where Les first worked with John Cleese who would later appear on *Sez Les*.

Roy appeared in the next seven series of *Sez Les* finishing with a New Year special. The pair also appeared in *All Star Comedy Carnival* (a seasonal special with Jimmy Jewel, Jimmy Tarbuck and Yootha Joyce), *Holiday with Strings* (a play with Mollie Sugden, Frank Thornton and Patricia Hayes), *Sounds Like Les Dawson* (with Olivia Newton-John), *Christmas Box* (co-written by Eric Idle), *Dawson's Electric Cinema* (with Daphne Oxenford – and Les's son Stuart as a young

Les), *Dawson's Weekly* (a series of plays featuring Patsy Rowlands, Avril Angers, Richard Vernon and Julian Orchard), *The Les Dawson Show* (written by Barry Cryer and David Nobbs and featuring Joan Sanderson and Cleo Laine), another *Christmas Box* (this time with Julian Orchard and Kenny Ball), *The Galton and Simpson Playhouse* (another series of plays by the legendary writers with guests Arthur Lowe, Leonard Rossiter, Frances de la Tour, Richard Briers and John Bird) and *Dawson and Friends* (another series with Hinge and Bracket, Kathy Staff, Willie Rushton and Dana) before they moved to the BBC with *The Dawson Watch* (three seasons co-starring Vicki Michelle, Bella Emberg and Gordon Peters), *The Les Dawson Show* (five seasons with Vicki Michelle, David Jason, Lulu, Eli Woods and The Roly Polys) and *The Funny Side of Christmas* (another seasonal special with Frank Muir, Ronnie Barker, Wendy Craig and Paul Eddington).

That's quite a list – but add to that innumerable radio shows including *Listen to Les* for BBC Radio 2 throughout the 1970s and 80s, guest spots, theatre appearances and cabarets (across the UK and even in the South of France).

In 1984, to mark the theatre's 90th anniversary, they were asked to appear in summer season at the Blackpool Grand Theatre. It was a venue both had fond memories of, and it would turn out to be a record-breaking season. *Laugh with Les* was produced by legendary producer Billy Marsh (the man who discovered Norman Wisdom, Bruce Forsyth and nurtured Morecambe and Wise). Billy notoriously chain-smoked Senior Service (I remember sitting next to him at an opening night when you could smoke in theatres, and he never let up. We sat there in a thick blue haze, ash pouring down on our coats) and when he died his ashes were placed under the stage at the London Palladium. Bruce Forsyth once told me that above Billy's last resting place was a 'No Smoking' sign. Whether that's true or not I don't know but Bruce's ashes were also placed near the same point when he died.

The show featured The Roly Polys (who, by now, were popular members of the Dawson repertory company), Katie Budd (winner of *Opportunity Knocks* in 1977), The Jolly Brothers, Maurice Merry's Musicmakers, Ray Cornell's Wild Affair and Puppets on Parade. Les and Roy appeared in the guise of Cissie and Ada for one sketch during which Cissie had to enjoy a drink from Ada's hipflask. Roy had been suffering from a very heavy cold and was taking all kinds of linctus and embrocation, so he was already a bit groggy. Les took the opportunity to fill the hipflask with a variety of alcoholic beverages – rum and port at the matinee, whiskey and vodka for the evening and so on. This continued over a few days and got so bad that one night Roy couldn't negotiate the stairs on the set and didn't, much to Les's amusement, make it on for the finale.

They also did adverts – mostly famously the 'Naughty but nice!' campaign for cream cakes and then there were the Post Office commercials in 1991. However, although Cissie and Ada both appeared in cartoon form, Les had to record both voices as Granada TV refused to allow Roy to do them as he was under contract to *Coronation Street*. A shame.

Roy and Les's relationship off stage and screen was much the same as on. When they started working together Roy appeared in lots of different sketches playing everything from vicars to doctors. Gradually, as Cissie and Ada became more popular, so he usually concentrated on that performance. The double-act came about because Les and Roy would chat to the studio audiences whilst lighting and cameras were being moved between sketches. Both had a love of Northern comics of the variety era – Robb Wilton, Frank Randle and Norman Evans in particular. They'd go into bits of their acts to fill the time and one day the producers remarked on how well these went down with the audiences. Why not include them in the show?

A lot of Les's material can be said to be a tribute to his favourite performers – there's definitely a bit of Frank Randle in lecherous Cosmo Smallpiece and you can spot WC Fields in magician Zebadiah Twine for example. Cissie and Ada were quite simply a tribute to Norman Evans' 'Over the Garden wall' routine in which he dragged up as a gossipy housewife, Fanny Fairbottom. They both lived in the era of thousands of women working in the mills who had to use exaggerated lip movements so that colleagues could lip read over the noise of the machinery (known has mee-mawing) and that very much became part of the act.

In the early sketches, where Les (Ada) would often wander off script, Roy (Cissie) doesn't say that much. Roy explained that this was because Les would prefer not to rehearse or learn the script too carefully. Instead, as a stand-up, he preferred to free-form it a bit and would often say to Roy just before filming ... 'We'll do the lobster gag, go onto the mother-in-law and finish with the chimp up the lamppost' or whatever.

Les knew what he meant but Roy, who was an actor rather than stand-up, learnt scripts religiously and didn't have a clue what Les had been talking about. They'd go for a take and Roy would wait for a point at which he felt comfortable to jump in. Roy was the 'feed' (as it's referred to in comedy) – the person who throws in the feed line which allows the comedian to get to the laugh-line. Later, as their relationship grew, Roy had heard the lobster gag a hundred times and knew the tag to the chimp up the lamppost then he could join in and enjoy the ride – and Cissie had more to say, and they shared more of the 'tags' to the jokes.

They loved making each other laugh. If you watch the Cissie and Ada sketches in particular, then you see what they do. Les would corpse (the term used for making a performer laugh) when he found food names funny. Roy would laugh at people's names. You often find in the sketches that Les will call Ada something like 'Ada Bernice Shufflebottom' or some such. That would get Roy going. Roy might invent names of cakes – 'Florrie's Cream lagoon' is one. Florrie being Roy's mum's name. Once they start to laugh, you see it build. The audience love it and laugh and then Roy and Les get worse. You can see that they loved each other and trusted each other even if the result was hysterics.

The last time they appeared on television together was *Coronation Street's 30th Birthday Special* in 1990. Hosted by Cilla Black, and with a surprise appearance by the now retired Doris Speed, who had played Annie Walker, the entire cast was assembled to watch the tribute show. In one sketch, performed live on the night, Roy is Alec Gilroy behind the Rovers' bar when Les comes in as Ada, looking for a job. There are a few in-jokes (Bill Waddington's lines being written on a beer mat for example) and a lot of the traditional Cissie and Ada stuff. It's a joy to watch.

175

When Les died, Roy was heartbroken. He was immediately flooded with offers from other comedians to re-create the Cissie and Ada act but he refused them all. As far as he was concerned the act was gone too. He often remarked that he'd over-heard some conversation in a café and he missed ringing Les to convey the line so that they might use it. The nearest he got to playing Cissie again was, perhaps surprisingly, when he appeared with the Birmingham Royal Ballet at the Birmingham Hippodrome. We had been at an awards ceremony when a man came for a chat – he ran the ballet company and he explained that each Christmas they performed a spoof version of the Nutcracker for charity. It was called *The Cracked Nut* and he asked if Roy would appear as Cissie.

I will always remember the couple of days we had there. For one thing, they sent a car to take us to Birmingham and the driver was so thrilled to have Roy to chat to that his driving went out of the window and we were beeped at and sworn at all the way as he cut people up, failed to indicate and even went down a one-way street the wrong way. He had no idea.

When we arrived at the ballet rehearsal rooms, we didn't know what to expect or indeed what was required. To our amazement there were wardrobe fittings and full rehearsals with the corps-de-ballet as Roy appeared in the Arabian Dance in full body make-up and bald cap, and as Cissie he emerged from the sorcerer's cabinet as if cleaning the loo. It was an amazing night.

Just one final tale of Les. Roy and I met with Les's wife Tracy for lunch one day in Lytham St Annes and afterwards we went down to the statue of Les which is situated in the gardens by the pier. As we approached, ahead of us were two ladies looking the statue up and down. 'No, I'm not keen,' remarked one to the other. 'At least Eric Morecambe has his leg up.' Very Cissie and Ada.

I must take you back to dear Kathy Staff, and her husband John. Kath's birth name was Minnie Higginbottom and she was born in Dukinfield not far from where we lived. She worked as a secretary whilst appearing with local amateur societies then she took the plunge and gave up the day job to join a repertory company. It was whilst appearing in Llanelli that she met John, who at that time was attending university studying pure mathematics. He would later become a teacher. Kath chose her stage name as Katherine Brant. She liked Katherine – in fact one of their daughters was called Katherine and she was passing a shop called Brant's on the bus when trying to decide on her stage name. As simple as that. Then marriage changed it to Staff and then her agent mentioned that everyone was calling her Kathy so that was that. Kathy Staff she became.

Everyone remembers Kath as Nora Batty in *Last of the Summer Wine*, Mrs Blewitt in *Open All Hours* or as Doris Luke in *Crossroads* but she also appeared in *Coronation Street* as an extra and then in a number of speaking roles, including an applicant for Ena's job, before landing the regular part of Vera Hopkins, mother of Tricia Hopkins played by Kathy Jones. The family ran the corner shop for owner Gordon Clegg (Bill Kenwright) between 1974 and 1975. She was forced to leave the shop, and the show, when she joined Summer Wine.

We saw Kath and John a lot – they lived opposite my business for a while and then moved just a few doors down from our home. We were always popping in and out of each other's houses for a cuppa and a catch-up. Kath and John used to drive all over the place seeing friends in shows. They were very loyal. We were both very friendly with Lynnette McMorrough (*Crossroads*' Glenda Brownlow) and we often bumped into each other at theatres Lynette was appearing in. Here's a fact you'd never think was true - I actually gave Lynette away when she married actor Nick Wilton – a great honour. Lynette is one of the funniest, warmest people I know. She tells some funny stories – there's the one of her meeting *Crossroads* producer Jack Barton at a cast party. She had just filled her mouth with prawns when he tapped her on the shoulder. She turned round with her face full of crustaceans. She didn't last much longer in the show! Then I often chuckle when I recall her tale of a studio car being sent to collect her from home early one morning. She was running late and rushed out of the house and jumped into the back of the car. 'You'll need to put your foot down!' she instructed the driver. He refused and there was a stand-off. It transpired that her car was the one behind, and this poor chap, who was just parked up, thought he was being car-jacked.

I was invited to the Staff's golden wedding dinner and was seated with Bill and Dora Bryan (Bill: 'I've driven up from Brighton without taking a break' Me: 'Oh Bill, that's too much for you!' Bill: 'It was fine – someone suggested a drink to have before we set off. It was called Red Bull and I didn't even notice there was any other traffic on the road.') and Ernst Walder. Ernst had appeared in *Castle Haven* with Kathy and Roy. He is also remembered for his role of Ivan Cheveski, Elsie Tanner's son-in-law, in *Coronation Street*. He was also, when the Street started, Tony Warren's partner. By the time we met he had gone back to live in his native Austria where he was making cuckoo clocks. He told me all about his life. He had been conscripted into the Nazi army and whilst serving in Italy made his escape, crossing the snowbound mountains into Austria with the help of farmers and the like. His tale would have made a movie script. As he made it back into his native country, he collapsed by the roadside, utterly exhausted, but was lucky enough to be found by a woman who nursed him until he was fit enough to continue home. He was later arrested for helping refugees out of the country and escaped himself, again, from the Russian zone and made his way to England. This came back to haunt him when, in 1966, he was flying to West Berlin to film *The Quiller Memorandum.* His plane landed in the Russian-controlled sector and he was questioned for many hours before being driven to Checkpoint Charlie and released. It was an amazing story.

Kath and John were very religious and had been members of St Mark's Church in Dukinfield all of Kath's life. When she died, in 2008, a blue plaque was placed there (unveiled by Roy) and a stained-glass window also commemorates her. A lovely tribute. I, quite often, go and visit her and John's grave and have a natter. Oh, and I always think of Angus Lennie, who played Shughie McFee in *Crossroads* with her. He once said: 'Kathy Staff is always encouraging me to be a better person – it's lovely, but I just don't want to be one!'

Talking about Ernst has just reminded me of a lovely encounter with actress Joan Francis who played Dot Greenhalgh in *Coronation Street,* Elsie Tanner's best friend and sidekick and one of Pat's too. Joan appeared in the show for nine years on and off, but she knew many of the cast – Pat, Doris, Peter

Adamson and so on from her days in repertory theatre. I often tell the tale of her baking. She used to produce copious cheese and onion pies for the cast and one day someone commented on her fabulous pastry. 'Ah,' she replied, 'I love making pastry. It's so good for getting the dirt out from under your fingernails.' Yuk!

The aforementioned Ken Parry recalled having Joan and Dorothy Squires at his flat for dinner. They both liked a drink, or ten, and by 3am he was fed up with the two of them – and they wouldn't leave. Suddenly Dot wanted to cook sausages and bacon, so they all went off to the kitchen. 'They would not stop bloody singing and going on with themselves,' Ken told me. 'So, as they stood at the hob cooking, I stood behind them and lit matches slowly setting fire to each of the beaded tassels on their dresses. Suddenly Dot turned and saw what I was doing. They were stunned. That shut the buggers up and they never came again!'

]

TWELVE – EAMONN, CYNTHIA & MANDY

I have already mentioned my brief role in Paula Tilbrook's *This Is Your Life* – that was the only one I actually appeared on. I was called upon to provide background information on a couple of other subjects including Anne Kirkbride and I always felt torn in doing so.

Roy hated the show as I've said. He was asked to appear on it, as a guest, many times and he usually refused. There were a few exceptions – Les Dawson's of course, Anne Kirkbride's, Gretchin Frankin's, Bill Tarmey's and Kathy Staff's – and Tony Warren's. And he broke another rule for that one - Roy had filmed in people's houses many times, you know, when people had hired out their homes for location shoots. He always said that, as a result, he would never let a film crew in his own home. Tony's tribute was the sole exception, and he filmed his contribution in the conservatory.

Actors tend to be very private people. *This Is Your Life* therefore could throw them over the edge. There are many tales of actors being taken ill after the show – Kathy Staff came out in shingles as did Roy, Jill Summers fell ill, Richard Thorp is another. Having your life unveiled, without you knowing what's coming, in front of a studio audience, your colleagues – and the nation - is too much to bear.

Roy's came about in 1987 because the producers were planning to surprise footballer Gary Lineker, then playing for Barcelona, but Gary was having a rare loss of form and it was decided to shelve his so they turned to Roy who had, as Alec, not long married Bet. Hence the secret code 'wedding' being used. The researchers, I'm told, contacted Roy's agent who told

182

them that Roy wouldn't like it. They contacted Roy's parents who said that he wouldn't like it – and anyway he didn't actually watch the show. They had to produce a show and they needed a subject I suppose so the planning continued.

Bill Podmore, *Coronation Street* producer, was in on it. The problem was that the date of the 'hit' was 13th October (the show was due to air a week later) and Roy would be on a well-earned holiday in Spain with one of the show's writer, Tom Elliott and his wife Beryl. A secret plan was hatched – Bill would wait until Roy had enjoyed a couple of days of his break and then telephone him to tell him that a scene had been accidentally wiped and he had to fly back to re-record it. He could then return to Spain for the rest of his holiday. And that's what happened. Roy wasn't pleased of course but he agreed to fly back to the UK.

On the first 'plane to London he asked for a gin and tonic. He was served a glass of tonic. The same thing happened the next time he asked. He was now getting miffed. Later the steward wrote to him to explain that he was in on the plot as well and had been told not to allow Roy any alcohol. At Heathrow he had to change for a 'private plane' but he was sent to the wrong terminal and everyone he rang for help was engaged or not answering. He was slowly losing his temper with Granada's inefficiency. Eventually he boarded the tiny aircraft and they set off into strong winds. Roy was sick. At Manchester Airport there was a car waiting. The driver opened the back door, but Roy always liked to travel in the front. The driver refused to allow him to sit in the passenger seat. The truth was that the front passenger footwell was full of technical gubbins including a microphone which Bill Podmore was listening into.

The car set off and after a while, on a country lane, the driver said: 'Oh look, there's Julie Goodyear's Rolls Royce parked up there, she must have come to meet you!' but Roy couldn't understand that as Julie wasn't in the 'wiped' scene so he told the driver not to stop and get him to the studios as quickly as he could. The poor driver didn't know what to do of course – he had been instructed to stop the car no matter what. There was an AA van parked by Julie's car and Eamonn Andrews was dressed up as a patrolman with his head in a smoky engine. At first Roy's car drove past throwing the *This Is Your Life* crew into chaos but then it stopped and reversed.

Roy got out of the car, Eamonn appeared to declare: 'Roy Barraclough this is your life!' to which Roy said: 'Oh no it's not!' and got back into his car. That was edited out of course. Everyone tried to persuade him, but he was not, at first, for turning.

Back at Granada Roy only agreed to do the show when he found out that his parents were there. He certainly didn't let things lie. When Bill Podmore came through the doors Roy told him that he could tear his *Coronation Street* contract up – he was quitting. He did the show and then took the microphone from Eamonn and told the studio audience the full story.

Although Roy rarely gave press or TV interviews, he did pop up now and again on things like *Noel's House Party* in which he played the semi-regular part of Wrinkly Bottom's resident undertaker, *Blankety Blank* with both Les and Paul O'Grady and *Surprise Surprise* with our Cilla. He appeared on *Loose Women, Lorraine* and *The One Show* once each and then only because it was part of his contract to promote something or other. He was so shy that he would never have done them otherwise. *This Morning* had to be done twice.

The first time he was just about to be introduced when news came through that the Labour leader John Smith had died so the show was taken off air and replaced with the news. Roy was sent home and had to go back another day, quite understandably.

He pressed the button for one of the early *National Lottery* draws when Mystic Meg took part. During the afternoon there was a rehearsal – and the numbers used by the camera crew's syndicate came up. Oh dear! They could have been millionaires had it been live, but they had to continue with their work and grit their teeth. Mind you, one or two did suggest editing in the rehearsal day to the night's show. I would have been tempted too.

Cynthia Payne crossed our paths now and again. I think the first time we met her was at the home of one of our friends when she was staying with him. Cynthia, as you might know, was known as 'Madam Cyn' after her home in Streatham, south London, was raided by the police in the late 1970s. She had been holding parties, as she called them, involving young women and older men and her guestbook included politicians from all parties, judges and goodness knows who. During the raid, according to Cynthia, 55 men and 17 girls were in the house. There was a newspaper cartoon at the time of a chap in one bedroom being handcuffed and asking for his solicitor. Who was in the next bedroom. Cynthia accepted payment in Luncheon Vouchers (like gift vouchers) which may, or may not, have avoided taxation. She was sent to Holloway prison for eighteen months but served four.

Cynthia became something of a celebrity although she once told me that to avoid embarrassment for her family she'd changed her name. I didn't quite understand the logic, because 'Payne' was actually her real name but it was just spelt differently - 'Paine' - so I'm not quite sure what difference it made. She'd always had a desire to enter show business and now she had her chance – and she milked it for all it was worth God love her - appearing on chat shows, joining the after-dinner speaker circuit and even standing for parliament under her 'Payne and Pleasure' party banner.

We bumped into her at various events including Crufts - would you believe? The last time we saw her we were all guests at a reception at 10, Downing Street during the era of Tony and Cherie Blair. As we guests all lined up to go through the security office at the bottom of the street Cynthia linked my arm. 'We'll say we're a couple,' she smiled. As the policeman checked her bag, she looked him right in the eye and demanded to know if he was one of the coppers who'd raided her house. He explained that no, he'd never done so. 'Oh well, you're always welcome!' she smiled. She once said that she could look at a heterosexual man and instantly know if he was straight, kinky or just hard work.

In her hefty handbag she always carried press cuttings and photographs wrapped in plastic bags and she needed no encouragement to produce them. She would regale you with tales of her extraordinary life whether you asked or not. She had to put a sign in her bathroom asking guests not to have sex in there. 'Oh, it was dreadful you know. Someone once pulled the sink off the wall, so I had to stop 'em.' There were the pictures of elderly men in French maid's outfits. 'If you ever need a cleaner let me know. He pays you. All you have to do is give him a kick and off he goes.' Or the photo of a man lying on his back on her floral carpet covered in dust. 'Oh, that was my bank manager. He used to come round and pay to have the contents of the Hoover bag shaken on him. Loved it!'

That night at 10, Downing Street we were kept waiting around because Tony was involved with a crisis so Cherie had to deputise, and she was at another function in Wembley so we had to wait about until her return. Eventually we were lined up and shown into a room in pairs. Cynthia produced a copy of the famous Luncheon Voucher and announced to Cherie that she'd been one of her best earning girls! Oh dear! As we left word came down that they didn't want Cynthia having a photo in front of the famous black doors but that didn't stop her. No one ever stopped Cynthia Payne doing what she wanted to.

A group of us went on to The Ivy for dinner and I was seated next to Cynthia. Rumour spread that Tom Cruise was about to arrive so, handbag at the ready, off she went to assail him with tales of her past. 'He's ever so small so I'll have to go and keep a look out for him. I'm very big in Hollywood!' and off she went. Indeed she was – her life told in two films *Personal Services* and *Wish You Were Here*. She died in 2015. On her coffin sat the word 'sex' in flowers and actors dressed as policemen and French maids lined the route as *Bring Me Sunshine* played her into the crematorium. And in my wallet, even today, is the laminated Luncheon Voucher she gave me. On the back it reads in her hand: 'To Mark, thanks for all the past custom, Cynthia.'

The year before Cynthia died Mandy Rice-Davies passed away.   Mandy, along with Christine Keeler, was at the centre of the Profumo affair which discredited the government of 1963. Roy appeared with her in a theatre tour and he always recalled, whilst appearing in Scarborough, that he was walking past the theatre where a large poster of the two of them was on display. An elderly couple were stood there, and the man was pointing at the poster. 'What about seeing this?' the chap asked his wife. 'Never! She brought down the government, I'm not having you go anywhere near her!'

Over the years I've been asked to do everything from teaching a reality star how to do pantomime acting, writing speeches and extra bits of business for shows, I've even worked with a magician on staging his act. The strangest request to help out some performers came when I was directing a show in London. I was approached by a very handsome young man who explained that he was a trainee doctor and that he was involved with an end of term – well, he described it as a 'variety show'. For some reason, that I forget now, the director had withdrawn, and they wanted someone to go along to rehearsals and tell them whether it was any good.

I agreed and turned up on a bitterly cold night at a hall in central London. I sat there with my notebook in my hand to cast an eye over this 'work in progress' starring lots of trainee doctors. It started with a song and dance number which was hilariously satirical and very well sung. Then a sketch set in a doctor's surgery. Another song and then a sketch based around men visiting a brothel and catching various embarrassing medical conditions. The conclusion involved several young men fleeing the brothel during a police raid. Each of the junior doctors playing these customers suddenly appeared from behind a curtain absolutely stark naked.

This was followed by a song and dance number with lyrics about erectile dysfunction. Again, this was performed naked. I'd never seen anything like it – but

I persevered. There wasn't much spent on the costumes I can tell you! I did go along to see the actual performance and with the addition of lighting and the odd carefully timed black-out it wasn't perhaps as 'in your face' as it had been in the rehearsal room. It was quite an extraordinary show – and I've always remembered it when I've been sitting in front of a doctor. They're not as innocent as they look you know.

THIRTEEN – BROADWAY & BLACKPOOL

We often went to New York to see shows. It was our favourite thing – have a week there and try and see two shows a day. As such I've seen many, many famous faces, and Broadway legends, performing live. Angela Lansbury, Tom Bosley, Rebecca Luker, Roger Bart, Megan Mullally, Tommy Tune, Sutton Foster, Andrea Martin, Patti Lupone, David Cassidy, Catherine Zeta Jones, Nathan Lane, Quentin Tarantino, Kelsey Grammer, Debra Monk, David Hyde Pierce, Audra McDonald, Brian Stokes Mitchell, Marin Mazzie, Gary Beach, Fred Applegate, Debra Monk, Lou Diamond Phillips, Chita Rivera, Julie Andrews, Tony Roberts, Brian D'arcy James, Matthew Morrison, Morgan Freeman, Bernadette Peters, Jim Dale, Leslie Uggams, Frances McDormand, Linda Eder, Tony Randall, Jack Klugman – and many more.

When Daniel Craig and Hugh Jackman starred in the Broadway play *A Steady Rain* in 2009 we were invited to attend the opening night. We decided to make a week of it which involved seeing lots of shows, lunching with Millicent Martin, who was also there for the opening night, and catching up with friends.

A Broadway opening night is rather a grand affair. Firstly, the street the theatre is on is closed to traffic with New York cops waving you through if you are lucky enough to have a ticket and secondly, as the curtain falls at the end and the cast take their bows, the waiting press photographers rush down the aisles to grab some shots. As we left to make our way to the after-show party a couple of blocks away we followed Whoopi Goldberg. There was a cameraman harassing her whilst broadcasting live. She must have been furious but maintained a polite manner until he said that the interview was over. Then she rightly let rip. Roy sympathised and she walked with us the rest of the way.

When we arrived at the very upmarket Harvard Club a British chap asked for Roy's autograph and Whoppi was then curious to know who he was. Trying to explain Cissie and Ada to anyone who's never seen them is a trial. The beautiful room was soon full of celebrities – some we didn't recognise but others such as Jerry Seinfeld, Live Schreiber, Barbara Cook, Joel Grey, Matthew Morrison, Matthew Broderick, Jeff Goldblum, David Schwimmer, Naomi Watts, Rupert Murdoch – and Harvey Weinstein (not quite as infamous as he is now) were instantly recognisable. It was a very lavish affair and unlike any opening night I have ever been to here in the UK. And I've been to a few.

It was quite odd the number of places where Roy was recognised. We got off a cruise ship in Auckland, New Zealand one rainy day. We crossed the road and an elderly priest came running over to us. He was a big fan of Alec Gilroy's. Something similar in Tahiti and on the island of St Helena in the middle of the South Atlantic off the coast of south-western Africa, would you believe?

A slight diversion, again, to Hawaii. We flew into Honolulu one New Year's Eve's arriving at the Royal Hawaiian Hotel, known to all as the 'Pink Palace'. Anyway, we were greeted in the reception by staff proffering pink floral leis and coconut cocktails. It was all done with a degree of solemnity. They then sat us down and went to announce our arrival at the front desk. I could see a lot of chatter and pointing and then these two ladies returned and whipped the flowers from around our necks with less solemnity and more brutality. It turned out that we weren't expected. Arrangements were made to find us a room in another hotel, and we were asked to leave. After a couple of days, the Royal Hawaiian realised there had been a mistake – on their part. We were whisked back in a stretch limo and the same young ladies went through the ceremony, with poker faces, again!

When we were crossing the Atlantic on the Queen Mary 2 one time, we were sat in a lounge having a cuppa when a lady asked if she could sit with us. It was legendary film star Jane Russell, not that we recognised her immediately. Again, she was a delight and chatted away about her career which included roles in *Johnny Reno* and *Gentlemen Prefer Blondes*. She told us all about her time with legendary producer Howard Hughes. Hughes signed her up for seven-years and in 1947 she made her first movie for him, *The Outlaw*, about Billy the Kid. Hughes was determined to show off Russell's voluptuous figure, so he designed her a carefully constructed underwired bra. Jane told us that Hughes was very proud of this contraption, but she found it too uncomfortable to wear so she didn't actually do so. Instead, she padded her own bra with tissues and pulled the straps up tightly. It's amazing who you get to talk to at sea – and the topics discussed! Jane died a couple of years later aged 89.

Someone else we met at sea was Gerald Dickens, the great, great grandson of writer Charles Dickens. Gerald performs his famous ancestor's work all over the world on land and sea. The first time we saw him it was on a Christmas cruise, and he gave his one-man performance of *A Christmas Carol*. He creates the scenes using just a handful of props and he evokes every single character beautifully. As he acted out the arrival of the Ghost of Christmas Past so a lightbulb blew with a loud bang. Quite an unexpected effect.

I was thrilled a couple of years ago when Gerald agreed to perform *A Christmas Carol* as a fund-raiser for my local hospice at the Hyde Festival Theatre. Not only did he stay with me but I had the privilege of introducing the performance. We didn't have any exploding light bulbs, but we did have an enraptured audience.

Liliane Montevecchi is someone you may not have heard of but my goodness, what a fire cracker she was. Liliane had an amazing life – prima ballerina, Broadway star, film actress … let me tell you about her. One tale that she told in great detail was of her first visit to London from her native France. Her aunt was a costumier and Liliane and her parents were met at Southampton by a chauffeur-driven Rolls Royce with two Afghan hounds in the back. How decadent! Her aunt was working on Olivier's *Hamlet* at the time, just after the war, and young Liliane (she would have been in her teens) was thrilled to have lunch with Laurence Olivier himself and discuss the theatre with him. It was that conversation which set her on the path into show business.

When she joined MGM (she was one of the last to be signed to a seven-year contract) she began a friendship with Grace Kelly which led to her being asked to perform at her wedding to Prince Rainier III in 1956 (she had already performed at Prince Rainier's coronation in 1949). She appeared in countless films including *Daddy Long Legs* with Fred Astaire ('I did a beautiful dance with Fred – but it was cut from the movie darling!') and Leslie Caron, *King Creole* with Elvis Presley ('He was so sweet but surrounded by all his chums with greasy hair and faces covered with pimples!) and *The Young Lions* with Montgomery Clift, Dean Martin and Marlon Brando ('He taught me how to act!'). Amongst her friends were Gene Kelly, Elizabeth Taylor, Clark Gable and Andy Warhol who even painted her. She then joined the company of the famous Follies Bergere before heading back to the States. I always remember her story of appearing in a Broadway production, I think it was *Nine*, for which she won a Tony, and a fan sent her champagne every night with notes begging to meet her. She constantly refused. Then he sent her a red Ferrari. She still refused. Then there were tales of mobsters asking to her to hide diamonds in Las Vegas. She was amazing.

She high-kicked into our lives in 2003 when she was cast with Roy, Oliver Tobias, Josh Dallas, Nick Winston and Lara Pulver in the 50th anniversary revival of *The Boy Friend*. It was a fabulous production which started life at Windsor and then did a national tour. Towards the end of the tour there was talk of it going into the West End but alas, during the week at High Wycombe, the financial wheels came off and the tour collapsed in some acrimony.

In 2022 the impressionist and actor Jon Culshaw invited me to the Lowry to see his one-man play *Les Dawson Flying High*. In it he played Les – and Roy. I was quite nervous actually – what if I didn't like it? It's always difficult seeing friends in something that you don't think's very good – what do you say when you go back stage? Roy always used to declare: 'Well, what about you!' In actual fact I thought it was very good. Jon had some other friends in that night including actor John Thompson so we all went back to his dressing room and had a couple of drinks, but Jon asked me to wait so that we could talk about the show, which we did after everyone had left. Anyway, we chatted for quite a while and when we went to leave, we found we were locked in. Good job I'd liked it, wasn't it? We could have had a blazing row and then been locked in the theatre over night! Now, there's an idea for a play.

Back to *The Boy Friend* - before the financial difficulties it was a blissful time and Liliane brightened things considerably. She stayed with us from time to time, but she was obviously used to being treated as the star. A couple of weeks before the show played Bradford she decided that she would like to go there to find a suitable hotel in which to reside so off we went. Roy drove with me in the front passenger seat and madam lying across the back wearing full make-up, long scarlet dress (she nearly always wore red) and a feathered turban confection on her head. She was every bit Old Hollywood. We stopped for lunch en route and she insisted on going behind the bar to teach the staff how to make her favourite drinks. Her delightful husky French accent and theatrical style gathered an audience and she delivered a masterclass in creating signature cocktails.

In Bradford, we took her to the Midland Hotel, a Victorian station hotel, which had just been restored at some considerable cost. In glided the tall, willowy figure, trademark red feathers shaking about atop her head as she spoke. She demanded to see all the rooms and the manager duly obliged. I think he was a bit stunned. We trouped from one to another and they were each dismissed by a flick of an elegant hand. Then we found it – a suite she was happy with. As long as they moved the furniture from another room into there. She then telephoned Arlene Dahl to tell her she had found a room. Arlene, another Hollywood star and successful businesswoman, insisted on speaking to Roy and thanking him for looking after Liliane. It was an adventure into another world.

Sandy Wilson, the show's composer, also became a friend. Sandy wrote the show for the Player's Theatre in 1953. Its success resulted in a longer version opening at Wyndham's Theatre which ran for over 2000 performances. Then it opened on Broadway starring Julie Andrews in her Broadway debut alongside Millicent Martin and Moyna Mcgill, Angela Lansbury's mother.

Sandy was a great teller of tales too. 'The first time I went to New York they shot the President as I landed. Not a good start. They closed the airport and all the exits, so I went to the Algonquin Hotel where I had dinner and do you know what, no one was bothered at all. Life continued.'

When the show was in Blackpool I drove Barbara Knox over to see it. *The Boy Friend* was the show in which she made her professional debut at the Oldham Coliseum (if I remember correctly another actress jealously cut the crown out of her straw hat). We had a wonderful evening and afterwards went to The Imperial Hotel where Roy and Liliane were staying. Roy had the Prime Ministerial suite and Barbara, Roy, Liliane and I enjoyed a supper of smoked salmon and champagne into the early hours of the morning.

When the *Boy Friend* tour abruptly came to an end many of the cast departed for London. Liliane boarded the train and then checking her bags couldn't locate her purse so she, no doubt in grand theatrical style, pulled the emergency cord and the train came shuddering to a halt. All the passengers around her hunted through her hastily packed bags until the purse was found and then she lowered the window and hung out shouting 'Take this train to London!' Her life was a Hollywood musical.

A few months later we received an invitation from the palace in Monte Carlo inviting us to a summer ball. Sadly, we had to reply that we'd be in Darlington that night – but it was nice to be invited! Liliane died in 2018 and I was delighted to read that during her stay in hospital she insisted on wearing high heels over her hospital bootees.

FOURTEEN – JULIE, DORIS & BET

One of my closest friends is Julie Goodyear.

I often spoke to Julie on the telephone when she would call for Roy but think the first time we properly met was at the Oldham Coliseum when she was filming for a documentary on her life. Julie has presence. She and Roy were similar in that they were utterly professional about playing their roles (although Roy's boredom frequently led him to mess about a bit) and they had a similar sense of humour, but they were also polar opposites in other ways. Julie had a desire to stay on the show for a long time whereas Roy would only sign a six-month contract at a time and was always dreaming of doing other roles. Roy was also shy and quiet whereas Julie was very outgoing. Julie once told me that there was no point in entering a room if no one noticed you. We went for lunch one day in a local restaurant where I was a regular customer. Julie asked me if I could arrange a table in a corner with her back to the room and would it be possible for her to enter through a fire exit so that she could slip in and not be noticed. I spoke to the manager to arrange everything. When she arrived, I was there to open the door – in she swept - bee-hive on, layered in leopard print waving at everyone and going around all the tables for a chat. So much for the low-key entrance! But people love to meet her! She is, without doubt, a British TV icon.

When Bill Tarmey died, I arranged a chauffeur-driven car to take Roy and I, Julie, Scott and Julie's PA to the church. Again, it was one of those events with a long line of photographers waiting outside and Roy and Julie linked arms and gave them the shot they wanted – the Gilroy's back together. That was a bit of a theme really. After Roy had left the show, the first time, he was asked back to film Alec's granddaughter Vicky's wedding to Steve McDonald. Roy loved Chloe Newsome who played Vicky and treated her like she was his real family – we often travelled across the country to see her in plays and to take her out to eat. He also had a lot of time for Simon Gregson who played Steve – and it was for them really that he agreed to return for a few episodes.

The wedding scenes were shot at Dukinfield Town Hall on a Sunday morning but so many people and press turned out to watch that the script had to be hastily rewritten so that the exterior scenes took place inside. It was so bad that a sort of fence had to be erected and one lady even took payment from a tabloid photographer to let him go upstairs in her house and climb out of the bedroom window on to her roof to get a good shot. She forgot to warn him that her husband was on nights and asleep in his bed – he got quite a shock to find a tabloid photographer in his bedroom!

When I rang Julie to tell her that Roy had died, I asked if she would make a statement to the press which she did. 'I will treasure all the happy times we had working and laughing together. We were just like a married couple - crazy, I know, but true.'

It was true. On set they built an amazing working partnership. They were both perfectionists and spent lots of time working the Rovers set as if it was a real pub. A lot of their lines fitted around 'business' or actions. So, they might have a couple of lines and then serve, say Mike Baldwin, go to the back of the bar, pour his scotch and then have to time the walking back so that they arrived at the bar again to say their next line. There was a lot of choreography and timing to get right. They used to rehearse all that - always pour the drink properly and they liked to give the correct change.

They both always knew their lines and they always gave a lot of thought to what they'd be wearing. I well recall Roy searching in shops for a suitable coat or cardigan for Alec – and there were times when my ties were pressed into action. Vicky came home from Switzerland at one time and brought Alec a tie as a gift. The one the studio provided was a standard M&S tie, but Roy wanted something that Vicky would have been proud to buy so one of my best silk ones was pressed into action. I used to buy novelty ties to wear at theatre opening nights at the Coliseum – so if we were doing a play set in the USA I'd wear a stars and stripes tie or a nautical one for a show set by the sea. Alec followed suit and several ties with beer glasses, wine bottles or bunting were borrowed for Alec to wear in specific situations.

There's one notorious scene which Julie often talked about – a bedroom scene – where both Roy and Julie tried to 'corpse' each other. Roy went onto the set early and placed various props on the bedside cabinets to make Julie laugh. Julie then did the same not realising Roy had been there first. So, the Gilroy's bedside cabinets were awash with 'stud spray' and goodness knows what. Roy came on to the studio floor in his dressing gown and climbed into bed followed by Julie.

The scene started and the sound man then came forward to say he was picking up a buzzing sound on his headphones. A search ensued to find what could be causing it – Roy had put a sex toy under the covers on Julie's side. That was removed. Then the crew spotted the various products littered about the place and there was much laughter. They had to be removed. Then music. Julie was wearing musical underwear which played *The Only Way Is Up*. That finished everyone off. The director threatened them with the sack if they didn't get on and film the scene. I'd love to see the unedited footage.

In more recent years, after Roy's death, Julie and I became closer. We spoke regularly and she invited me to attend the ceremony at Rochdale Town Hall when she was given the freedom of the Borough. A friendship developed. But let's look back first. Julie was born in Heywood near Rochdale (she used to say that she never left and went to 'Cheshire' – always pronounced mock posh – because they never forgave Gracie Fields for leaving this part of the world) by her mother and her stepfather. They ran a pub in the town, the Bay Horse Hotel, and Julie often talked about being brought up there. She said that when she went behind the bar of the Rovers it felt natural, she was at home.

Julie's love life has led to acres of newsprint and shock headlines down the years – she married her first husband at her father's insistence as she was pregnant. However, they married for all the wrong reasons, and he left her, eventually emigrating to Australia. Her second marriage broke up on the wedding day when, at the reception, she discovered in no uncertain terms that he was gay. Her third was a long distance one to an American businessman. The fourth was to Scott, whom she met when he delivered cement to her new home. They dated for over a decade with him asking her to marry him every day and her refusing.

Julie started her career as a hand and foot model. 'I have very small hands and my feet are only size four, so I actually made more money than the very tall models,' she told me. She also started singing in and around the local pubs and clubs. 'I think it was at the Carlton. I was singing *Blue Moon* when this fella threw a meat pie at me. So, I picked it up and ate it. I was hungry. And I don't like waste, never have,' she said with a straight face.

Roy and Julie first met in 1966 when Pat Phoenix suggested she go and get some formal training at a repertory theatre and, I think, she pulled some strings to get her taken on at Oldham. Roy was in the acting company there at the time and Julie was employed as an assistant stage manager (ASM). There are lots of stories about her antics at the 'Rep'. The theatre was run by Carl Paulsen at the time, an idiosyncratic character. ASM's were responsible for organising props and helping run the show – which could be changing scenery, helping actors in and out of their costumes, prompting, whatever was needed. If you went up a grade, then you might be asked to play small speaking and non-speaking roles too.

There's a lovely story of Carl being upset at the quality of props on a set one day and calling the ASM on stage where she stood holding a tray. On it sat a collection of glassware from the set. 'This is what I'm talking about,' he started. 'Rubbish like this on my stage!' and with that he threw the whole thing into the air, shards of glass and pottery going everywhere. 'Now,' he said to the tearful ASM, 'you can go and explain to whoever you borrowed them from that you weren't doing your job very well.' 'Oh,' she replied,' but I borrowed them from your house.' Julie used to drive a sports car at the time which annoyed many of the actors who were on more money but couldn't afford such a luxury. It looked lovely but it was usually filthy, so the theatre cleaners cleaned it one morning. Well, half of it. As I've said before, Julie knew how to make an entrance and on her first day at the theatre she was sweeping the stage. Whilst wearing a mink coat!

Julie's duties included tidying the stage and keeping everything backstage neat and tidy. According to several people I've met down the years she didn't quite see it like that and if she was picked up on this, she would hand her broom to the actor concerned and suggest they got on with the cleaning instead. Barbara Knox once told me that she was starring in a play there which had a very dramatic scene set during a storm. She came off stage to find Julie 'creating' the rain effects with a bucket full of peas. Julie, whom she had barely met, looked her up and down and then handed her the bucket. 'Shake that!' she said before lighting herself a cigarette. Barbara said that she immediately knew that Julie would be a star one day.

On my office wall at the Coliseum used to hang a framed photograph from a production of the musical *A Funny Thing Happened on the Way to the Forum*. It was significant in that Julie who played a small walk-on part was in the picture – her blonde hair up and wearing a leopard-print bikini. Years later she showed me a picture of herself modelling at an even earlier age – again in leopard. This of course is something she carried over into the role of Bet Lynch – the earrings, the leopard, the big hair. Julie said that she and Tony Warren walked around Salford market and looked at real-life Bet's until they found her characteristics. Maybe. Maybe Bet was quite a lot of Julie. 'It's always been very kind to me' she once told me when I pointed to the various leopard print items around the house. 'And it's cheap.'

Julie explained the philosophy behind Bet. 'Tony Warren was obsessed with strong women – many gay men are, aren't they? – we were his drag queens. Bet was part strength, comedy, vulnerability, you see. The beehive, the leopard, the jewellery – you see thousands of drag queens looking like me – and bloody hell, they don't just look like me, they look *better* than me a lot of the time. Bet became a gay icon – look at Freddie Mercury in *I Want to Break Free* – what an amazing thing that is. Bet was my best mate too – she was my escape from my own personal problems. Bet always picked herself up and got on with life. She's a clown with a smile painted on.'

As a non-drinker when I visited what I dubbed 'Leopard-print Boulevard', her home in Heywood, I had tea whilst Julie always had a glass of her favourite fruity pink wine. My tea was served in a leopard-print tea pot, on a leopard-print tray with a leopard-print napkin and a leopard-print milk jug. My mug had Julie's photo on it and her famous line 'I've got tights older than you!' emblazoned across it. You could be in no doubt whose house it was.

We used to chat about Corrie of course and Julie had some fabulous tales. She was always close to Pat Phoenix and was no doubt influenced by the way Pat conducted herself. The Manchester Hollywood style rubbed off on her. Once Pat was criticised for dressing too smart as Elsie. Her reply was that she was trying to give hope to women of a certain age. Classic. Julie used to tell the tale of waiting at a bus stop to catch the bus to work. Suddenly a big cement lorry came to a stop. It was a friend of her dad's, and he offered her a lift so she clambered aboard and off they went. Half an hour later they pulled up outside Granada studios and Julie was clambering down from the cab when

Pat's Rolls Royce pulled into the bay in front. Pat climbed out and then surveyed Julie up and down. 'You'll kindly not try and upstage me again!' she admonished the younger actress.

In 1990 Roy and Julie were asked to switch on the famous Blackpool Illuminations – a great honour following in the footsteps of George Formby, Jayne Mansfield, Vi Carson, Ken Dodd, Gracie Fields, Sir Matt Busby, Doctor Who, the Muppets and Red Rum! To make sure they arrived in Blackpool on time, after a day's filming in Manchester, the decision was made to fly them by helicopter. Then someone suggested that perhaps they should have a helicopter each – after all, if the thing fell from the sky the show would lose a whole family. If one actor was lost it would be easier for the writers to work around it. So that's what happened - they flew separately from the car park of the Harry Ramsden's fish and chip restaurant.

John Stevenson had written a lovely routine for them all in rhyme and they were decked out in evening dress – Roy in a white tuxedo and Julie in a jewel encrusted red gown, diamante jewels and tiara. Afterwards they headed to the Town Hall for a civic reception at which, according to Julie, the mayor talked to her boobs all night. 'He never looked at my face once – all he had were eyes for Newton and Ridley!' she told me. Incidentally, in later years they actually had their images featured in the famous lights – and they were reproduced in wax for Louis Tussaud's Waxworks. I have an album of pictures showing the making – from lumps of clay to the finished models. There are a couple of very sinister looking pictures of the finished models which they used as that year's Christmas card with the slogan 'Bet and Alec – available for baby-sitting!' embossed on the picture.

When she first started in the show Julie liked to go on to the studio floor and watch the scenes she wasn't in being recorded. She watched the other actors and hoped to learn from them. One day, she was stood there in the dark behind the cameras when Margot Bryant who played Minnie Caldwell happened along. Margot swore like a trooper and loved a good row. So, there was Julie in the gloom and Margot crept up to her and whispered, 'What are you doing?' 'Watching,' replied Julie, 'Watching and learning.' 'But they're all f***ing useless!' replied Margot and shuffled off.

Doris Speed once said that Margot was 'As sophisticated, arrogant and provocative as Minnie could be docile.' She wasn't fond of children, but she did love cats once claiming that she owned a lucky tiger whisker which she'd gone into the cage with the beast to rescue. Tony Warren said that they had given Minnie her famous pet cat Bobby because someone had told him that they'd seen her in Venice feeding dozens of stray cats from dozens of tins of food. She was still wearing her prized mink coat.

After Julie had been in the show a while Doris Speed, who played Annie Walker, asked her to come to her dressing room at an appointed hour. Julie rang her mother for advice fearing that she was in trouble for something. Doris could be prickly at times and is famous for telling an extra who cast a shadow on her that the dole queues were full of people who had done the same. Eventually the time came, and Julie knocked and was admitted into the inner sanctum. 'Miss Speed, you asked to see me'. 'Yes, I have decided that you can call me Doris from now on dear,' the actress replied. 'You can go now.' But Julie couldn't do it, Miss Speed she remained for several more years yet.

Doris, incidentally, was like her alter-ego in many ways and she grew, according to those who worked with her, grander as the series went on, but she was also, in many ways, diametrically opposed to Annie in her views. Julie told me that when the cast were informed that the Queen and the Duke of Edinburgh were to visit the studios everyone was extremely excited. Whereas Doris didn't seem bothered at all. 'Mind you,' she said. 'She probably viewed it as meeting her equals.'

When Doris retired from the show a tabloid newspaper ran a scurrilous and nasty piece about her age. Doris had, as many actresses do, massaged her date of birth a little. She wasn't actually 69 as she claimed but was really 84. Something which should have been celebrated – instead she was ridiculed for it. They also claimed that she hadn't done any previous acting and that her parents hadn't been music hall artistes. Both untrue – after all, she first met Tony Warren whilst working with him.

Both Roy and Julie had a great deal of respect for Doris Speed and Arthur Leslie, who played Jack Walker. They felt that they played their roles in such a way that they were able to perform comedy and pathos and that they felt like a real couple. The Gilroy's tried to live up to that high bar.

Julie and I became very close, and I could see that she was becoming slightly forgetful. Stories she would once tell with great detail now became a little fuzzier. I asked her whether she'd like to record an interview for a radio show I was then hosting, and she agreed. We recorded it at her house with the two of us walking from room to room and talking about her life, using some of the pictures on the walls to trigger stories. It would prove to be the last interview she would grant.

Julie loves going out and about and of course, people recognise her all the time. She also still receives fan mail every week, years after she had stopped appearing in anything new on TV. But of course, her performances live on in repeats of *Coronation Street* around the world and in the UK.

We then realised that Julie's losses of memory weren't just fleeting, there was something more serious going on. The doctors diagnosed dementia.

Julie's desire to be out of the house continued and she and Scott started to become regulars at my garden centre so I now saw them most days. They decided that they weren't going to hide away; they were going to continue life as normally as possible, and adaptations had to be made.

Julie had, during lock down, donated a large amount of Bet's jewellery to Willow Wood Hospice in east Manchester that I, and Roy, had been involved in for years. This raised almost £20,000. The team there offered advice to Scott but could only do so much as they lived outside the hospice's catchment area.

We discussed releasing the news of her diagnosis to the public but wanted to hang on as long as we could. However, I was contacted by a newspaper to say that they had photographs of her and Scott out shopping. Something was obviously wrong, and they wanted a comment. So, the timing was taken out of our hands. Scott and I wrote a press release and decided that if it went out to all media at the same time then a line could be drawn under it. Everyone knew.

The reaction was amazing with thousands of wonderful messages being received from all around the world. Julie felt more able to go out and about without risking people taking photos or her risking being confused when chatting to fans. Another benefit was that the Alzheimer's Society reached out offering guidance. We often say that people *suffer* with dementia – that's not right. You have to adapt in order to *live* with it. There are several different types of dementia but it's basically a disease which affects the nerve cell's ability to communicate within the brain. Memory loss, confusion, changes in mood and language and understanding are the results. It's not a normal part of aging – it's a disease.

At the time of writing, it's estimated that some 900,000 people are living with dementia in the UK. Although it mainly affects those aged over 65 around 1 in 20 people are younger than that. Most types of dementia are non-hereditary – just because your parents or grandparents had it doesn't mean you will. It's mainly lifestyle-related – high blood pressure, smoking, drinking too much alcohol, inactivity, hearing loss and a poor diet are believed to be contributing factors.

In 2023 Julie decided to support the Alzheimer Society's Memory Walk in Heaton Park in Manchester. Scott, I and two of her carers went with her. Julie cut the ribbon to start the walk (and we completed it too!) and Scott agreed that a photographer could be there to capture the moment. Again, the reaction from her fans was amazing – and the charity benefitted from distributing the photos and the associated publicity. It was an honour to be there.

There was once a documentary called *The Truth about Julie Goodyear*. Whether it got to the 'truth' I don't know but there seems to have been a decades' long fascination with her, and Bet, and goodness me, acres of newsprint going over her life and loves. If I give a talk on my life and mention some of the people in this book – she is always the person people want to ask after. Julie is most definitely a legend – and I'm pleased to say that I think I'm one of the few people to be able to say that I really do know the real Julie Goodyear. Not the 'bold as brass' image she projected but a kind, sometimes vulnerable, rather gorgeous mate. A pal!

FIFTEEN - GOODBYE

My mobile 'phone rang at six thirty in the morning waking me up. I was told that Roy had passed away.

Roy died in Willow Wood Hospice, where he'd been founding patron, so immediately I had support from the team there who I knew well. I personally rang as many people as I could to tell them the news and I asked Julie Goodyear to make a public statement timed to hit the newsrooms minutes after the one from Roy's agent (which in fact I wrote). I hoped that this would stop them coming to me. I wanted to say nothing at that moment. To stay in the background. I've shared with you already what Julie's tribute said.

Corrie's Executive producer Kieran Roberts said: 'Roy was a delightful person as well as a wonderful actor and will be greatly missed by all of us connected with the programme. The fact that the character of Alec Gilroy was at the heart of the show for so many years and was held in such affection by so many fans is a tribute to Roy's genius, for drama as well as comedy.'

Beverley Callard, who played Liz McDonald, said: 'I will be forever indebted to Roy, he was one of the people who trained me in all the skills required for working in a long-running series like this.

'He almost got me sacked many times because he made me laugh so much. It was a joy to be in his company, he was one of the funniest people I knew, and he had the biggest heart. I feel honoured to have known and worked with him.'

Simon Gregson, who plays Steve McDonald, said: 'Roy's passing has come as a huge and sad shock. I learnt so much from Roy and was very proud to call him a friend. He was always lovely to me and I will miss him very much. He gave so much to entertaining people and will be very much missed.'

The next day we registered the death (a little strangely – this took place in Dukinfield Town Hall where Roy filmed Steve marrying Vicky and which was in effect, the last time Bet and Alec appeared together) and rather fittingly the registrar was wearing leopard-print - and had a first meeting with the undertaker who was called Julie. She was brilliant. I knew exactly what I wanted and she gave me confidence that she would oversee it precisely. I also wanted to write the service.

Over the next few days (the funeral was a week after Roy's death) I had many, many visitors and many cards and letters – quite a few from people I didn't know and who didn't know me. They found their way to my doorstep via the hospice or simply addressed to 'Family of Roy Barraclough, Manchester'. It was very touching.

The funeral itself went according to plan and was, by common consent, one of the best people had been to. Odd phrase that, isn't it? But I hope I wrote a service which reflected Roy.

Three days later I returned to work and it was only then that the loss started to kick in really. People tell you that there are five stages of bereavement – denial, anger, bargaining, depression, and acceptance. I was offered group counselling, but I decided against – I couldn't sit in front of a group of strangers and talk about my loss at that time.

Denial means, for some people, carrying on as if nothing has happened – or at least believing that the person is still there. I passed a car on the way to work one morning – it was Roy's car. Well, it wasn't - just one very like it. But seeing that car caused me to wonder whether it had all been true – was he really dead? What if it was a hoax? I went through everything in my mind. What if he'd staged it, what if – Reggie Perrin like – he'd sought to vanish? It could be a conspiracy. What if he just wanted to get away from me? Utterly illogical of course but that's what the mind does in times of extreme stress.

Anger is obviously a very logical emotion. Why has he died? Why did it have to be him? It can be that those left behind feel anger at the person who has died for leaving them – but that wasn't something I felt.

Bargaining is … well, we've all done it. Maybe a prayer to a 'greater being' saying if we do this or do that can we be rewarded in some way. 'If I become a kinder person, will you let me win the lottery?' Does that work? Who knows. Again, that didn't apply to me – that hoping to change something in that way, but I know people do it.

Depression. Yes, I certainly felt that, and I did sometimes, in the middle of the night, unable to sleep, plan how I would commit suicide. I didn't ever try but I think I came quite close on one occasion. I remember sitting in front of the computer screen in the early hours searching for advice, crying, and feeling desolate. I suppose the problem is when you don't seek the advice any more. I had some very black moments, but I didn't quite get to that point.

Acceptance. That wasn't the issue – it was working out who I was and coming to terms with being 'me' and not 'we'. About a year later I went on holiday with my sister and her family. When I got back, I locked the front door behind me, heaved the case onto the bed and collapsed. I cried and cried for ages, over an hour. I just lay on the floor crying uncontrollably. Not just crying actually – but howling, in pain. I'd had a lovely time but, I think, coming home to an empty house tipped me over the edge. I also felt guilty about having enjoyed myself.

I'm not sure how many people these stages apply to. It's a never-ending dance. A life-long state. It's not something you 'get over' and how can it be the same for each and every person. Your relationship with your loved one was unique to the two of you. That relationship carries with it history, shared experiences, and connection. It was something tangible to just the two of you and now it's gone. No more saying: 'Do you remember when…' Now I'm the only one who remembers it.

I speak to Roy, I talk about Roy, I smile at his picture. You're told to turn the grief into a positive, to find a new purpose. The worst for me is hearing something that Roy would have liked to have heard too – a bit of gossip, a funny story. But I still tell him.

A year or two after he died, I decided to have the house decorated and in preparation I had a clear-out. Now, I know some people find it difficult to throw away possessions – I'm not one of those, I'm not a hoarder. But there were things around the house such as his piano that really exercised me. I can't play the piano and it took up quite a bit of room so it made logical sense to give it away. I did in the end but it was tough – but Roy wasn't the piano and I didn't need the piano to remember him. But you know, it was still difficult to choose new wallpaper without thinking 'Would he like it if he were to come back?'

As I write this it's seven years since he died. I talk about him all the time – more so now because I can do it without bursting into tears. I have pictures of him and mementoes throughout the house. Bereavement is a tug of war – at one end, the loss, the pain, the space that never fills. At the other, the desire to keep going. Sometimes, a scent, a piece of music or a word jolts you to one end of the rope. Another moment - a dinner with family, a holiday – a hug. Yes, a hug pulls you in the other direction. But that tug of war never gets won.

Since Roy died tears come far more easily than they used to. If I watch a show in which someone is bereaved, I'm off. Not long after he died – a matter of weeks – I was driving somewhere with the radio on and one of those 'mystery voice' competitions came on. The voice was Roy's. That was tough, just like that out of the blue. But I now find solace in seeing him or hearing him (he's usually playing a part, so it isn't actually him, it's him pretending to see someone) – and I now know that I'm lucky to have that. I can stick in a DVD and there he is albeit playing a publican or a vicar or whatever. That's a privilege. I also started giving talks about him and Les and the reaction from people is amazing – their story and their material still entertains.

But the biggest thing I can do – any of us can do - is push on.

People don't knock on the door asking if you're lonely or if you want to talk, as a rule, so you have to get out there, increase your circle of contacts and friends, make yourself useful in some way. As you get older it becomes an increasing delight when someone younger asks for your help or advice. It's easy to become anonymous and I've found that volunteering for things fills up the hours very nicely.

Les Dawson used to tell the story of when he was working the clubs – before he became famous. He was playing South Wales and staying in a little lodging house with an elderly couple, the husband being blind. One night Les sat down with the man and discussed the world. What, asked Les, would the man wish for to make humanity better. 'Just be kind,' replied the man. Les never forgot that. It's a great mantra. Be kind to others – but, and this is just as important I think, be kind to yourself.

In early 2024 I was given the greatest honour of my life. I was asked by the Lord Lieutenant to become a Deputy Lieutenant for Greater Manchester. And my first engagement? – it took place at Dukinfield Town Hall where Bet and Alec made their last appearance together and where I registered Roy's death and where I went to the very first fund-raiser for the hospice and where Roy unveiled a blue plaque in honour of Kathy Staff and ..... somehow that felt right. It was like going home.

I'm lucky – so lucky – to have had the life I've had and to have met and worked with so many fabulous people. I'm blessed to have had friends like these and I hope that you have enjoyed ready about them.

I'm doing just fine thank you. I hope you are too.

With thanks to:

- Corriepedia
- Andrew Calder
- Tracy Dawson
- Chris Perry – Kaleidoscope Publishing
- Keith Boldy for permission to use his illustration of Julie Goodyear
- My family and friends

MARK LLEWELLIN

Mark studied performing arts in Yorkshire before moving to London to work at Mountview Theatre School and then London Transport where his duties included broadcasting travel information. For many years he was a director of the famous Oldham Coliseum Theatre where many stars began their careers – and some ended. He is joint Managing Director of Daisy Nook Garden Centre in Manchester.

Mark is a long-serving member of the voluntary team at Willow Wood Hospice in Greater Manchester and also a director/trustee of Your MCR which offers work experience and mentoring to media students whilst making a weekly on-line magazine programme and podcast focusing on Manchester's arts and heritage.

Mark's previous works include *They Started Here!*, *The World of Crime* and *Lights, Camera, Location!*

He is a supporter of The British Music Hall Society, Willow Wood Hospice and Highgate Cemetery.

In 2024 he was appointed a Deputy Lieutenant of Greater Manchester.

www.marktalks.co.uk

Printed in Great Britain
by Amazon

41908621R00126